Beyond Words

Beyond Words

Certificate reading and listening skills

Student's Book

Alan Maley and Alan Duff

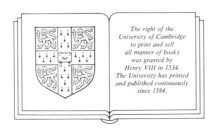

Cambridge University Press
Cambridge
London   New York   New Rochelle
Melbourne   Sydney

Published by the Press Syndicate of the University of Cambridge
The Pitt Building, Trumpington Street, Cambridge CB2 1RP
32 East 57th Street, New York, NY 10022, USA
296 Beaconsfield Parade, Middle Park, Melbourne 3206, Australia

© Cambridge University Press 1976

First published 1976
Sixth printing 1984

Designed by Ken Garland and Associates
Drawings by Daria Gan

First printed in Great Britain by
Cox & Wyman Ltd, London, Fakenham and Reading
Reprinted in Great Britain at the
University Press, Cambridge

ISBN 0 521 20985 4 Student's Book
ISBN 0 521 20986 2 Teacher's Book
ISBN 0 521 26348 4 Set of 2 cassettes

Copyright
The law allows a reader to make a single copy of part of a book
for purposes of private study. It does not allow the copying of
entire books or the making of multiple copies of extracts. Written
permission for any such copying must always be obtained from the
publisher in advance.

Preface

Beyond Words has two aims: to help you understand written and spoken English and to show you how to approach *any* text you come across, so that you will not be worried simply because you do not know a word or phrase.

In order to achieve these aims, the units have been arranged in pairs – Reading and Listening – each of which is on a similar topic. For example 'Battery buses' and 'Atomic cars' share a common theme – alternatives to petrol-driven vehicles. By *reading* about a topic first you will be better prepared to *listen* to something similar afterwards.

In the exercise material there are comprehension questions like those found in examinations such as the Cambridge First Certificate in English. But there are other, equally important exercises which will help you to see how a passage is put together. It is this ability which will be of great use to you in interpreting other texts. If you think of the text as a forest, we want you to be able to find your way through, and not necessarily to know the names of all the trees. If you are too worried by detail, you go round in circles; if you have a map, you can see where all the paths are.

A.M.
A.D.

Contents: Reading comprehension

Unit 1: Tall tales from the backwoods 3

Unit 2: The underworld 6

Unit 3: When you have an accident 10

Unit 4: Detectives' lives – fact and fantasy 13

Unit 5: Oil wealth flows up the Voe 16

Unit 6: Eyeless sight 20

Unit 7: Gold 25

Unit 8: Flicker 29

Unit 9: Shaka – King of the Zulus 32

Unit 10: Packaging 35

Unit 11: How lions hunt 39

Unit 12: Uri Geller's extraordinary powers 42

Unit 13: Battery buses 46

Unit 14: Shape and waves 49

Unit 15: Lost world of the Kalahari 54

Unit 16: Population growth and industry 58

Unit 17: Our first words 62

Unit 18: A sunrise on the veld 65

Unit 19: The secrets of sleep 69

Unit 20: The dangers of space 73

Contents: Listening comprehension

Unit 1: Three sacks of carrots   79

Unit 2: Darwin ruined by Cyclone Tracy   80

Unit 3: Speeding   82

Unit 4: The reality of being a detective   84

Unit 5: The curse of the islands   86

Unit 6: Colour and feelings   87

Unit 7: Pizarro and the Inca gold   89

Unit 8: A formidable sound   91

Unit 9: The stamping of the thorns   94

Unit 10: Recycling waste   95

Unit 11: How lions live   97

Unit 12: Telepathy   100

Unit 13: Atomic cars   102

Unit 14: What happens inside a pyramid   104

Unit 15: Up the creek   107

Unit 16: The year 2000   108

Unit 17: Learning to speak   109

Unit 18: Tiny killers on the march   111

Unit 19: Sensory deprivation in space   113

Unit 20: A near-disaster in space   115

Acknowledgements

Extracts are reproduced by permission of the following:

p. 3, Mr David Attenborough and *The Listener*; p. 10, Times Newspapers Ltd; p. 13, *TV Times* and Mr Peter Laurie; p. 16, Times Newspapers Ltd; p. 20, Dr Lyall Watson and Hodder & Stoughton Ltd; p. 25, *Newsweek*; p. 29, Dr Lyall Watson and Hodder & Stoughton Ltd; p. 32, *Look and Learn*; p. 35, Times Newspapers Ltd; p. 39, William Collins Sons & Co. Ltd; p. 42, The London *Daily Mail*; p. 46, Times Newspapers Ltd; p. 49, Dr Lyall Watson and Hodder & Stoughton Ltd; p. 54, Laurens van der Post and the Hogarth Press; p. 58, David Hay, *Human Populations* (Biology Topic Books, 1972), pp. 83, 85-6. Copyright © David Hay, 1972. Reprinted by permission of Penguin Books Ltd; p. 62, *The Observer*; p. 65, Curtis Brown Ltd; p. 69, *The Listener*, British Broadcasting Corporation and Dr Wilse Webb; p. 73, C. F. Stoneman, *Space Biology* (Biology Topic Books, 1972) pp. 64-5. Copyright © C. F. Stoneman, 1972. Reprinted by permission of Penguin Books Ltd.

Reading comprehension

Unit 1

Tall tales from the backwoods

I knew a man who collected English words. He lived in an upturned water tank in the middle of the Australian desert. Unbelievably hot. He was the official town librarian of one of these ghost towns in the outback of Australia. It was founded in the 1890s. People turned up and hammered wooden pegs into the sand and laid out boulevards and avenues. They built a jail and a huge corrugated-iron hotel. That's about all, except that someone down south had it on his books that this was an official town, and he sent a library to it, 3000 volumes and a sum of money as a salary for the librarian. This friend of mine, whose name was Roger, had been a *no-hoper*, as they say, wandering about the outback of Australia. He somehow discovered that there was money to be had there and, what is more, boxes of unopened books sitting in this deserted hotel.

He turned up there, got the job, and settled down in the hotel, to begin with. The hotel did, actually, just function: that is, it had half a dozen guests a year who would ride up on horseback, sleep on the floor for an evening, and then push off the next day. This was too much for Roger. It got in the way of his reading. So he took the immense water-storage tank, rolled it a mile into the desert, carried his books out there and lived inside it – so, as he said, 'I could get a bit of peace and quiet'.

Words were a fascination for Roger, and he used to sit in his tank, just thinking about words. If there was a pause in the conversation he would look at you and ask some such question as: 'D'you happen to know what "transubstantiation" is?' If you said you knew, he was very cast down, because he wanted to tell you.

One of his regular visitors was the government officer who went by every six months. Roger would ask him if he knew what a word meant, and then he would have to admit that he didn't, and Roger would be very pleased with himself. Taz, as his name was, got very fed up with this. So, on one occasion, before he went, he spent an evening with the Oxford English Dictionary. He rode in, tied up his horse and went in to see Roger, and Roger said: 'D'you happen to know what an "embolism" is?' and Taz said: 'No, I bloody don't.' Then Taz asked him: 'D'*you* happen to know what a "leotard" is?' Roger was upset to be asked a question. He said: 'A leotard? I think I saw the skin of one once.' And Taz said: 'You bloody didn't.' So Roger said: 'Well, what is a leotard?' Taz said: 'I'm not going to bloody tell you!.' He got on his horse and rode off and went to sleep in the desert five miles away.

Some time later he was suddenly woken up by a steely grasp on his coat. Hands picked him up bodily from the ground and held him in the air and shook him. He opened his eyes and it was Roger with his eyes glinting in the moon light, staring at him, and saying: 'What's a bloody leotard?'

(From an article by David Attenborough in *The Listener*)

Reading comprehension: Unit 1

Mutiple choice

Read the passage carefully, then answer the following questions.
Choose the response which best reflects the meaning of the text.

1 The outback town was given a library because
a) it was expanding rapidly.
b) Roger was a collector of English words.
c) a government official thought it necessary.
d) the people of the town had requested one from the government.

2 Roger did not stay long at the hotel because
a) it was forced to close down.
b) there were too many guests.
c) he wanted more time for reading.
d) he was used to living in the desert.

3 Taz, the government officer,
a) was fascinated by Roger's encyclopaedic knowledge.
b) felt sorry for Roger.
c) got tired of being asked the meaning of words.
d) was ashamed at knowing less than Roger.

4 When Taz asked his question, Roger
a) thought he knew the right answer,
b) pretended not to know the right answer.
c) admitted at once that he did not know the right answer.
d) deliberately gave a stupid answer.

5 The reason Roger went into the desert after Taz was that
a) he wanted to murder Taz.
b) he was desperate to know what the word meant.
c) he thought Taz had been trying to fool him.
d) he had suddenly remembered the answer to the question.

True or false?

Without looking back at the text, decide whether the following statements are true or false.

1 The people of the outback town were extremely grateful for the gift of 3000 books.
2 Roger was a trained librarian.
3 The hotel had very few guests.
4 Roger had the water tank carried out into the desert.
5 Roger was dismissed from his job as librarian.
6 When Roger asked people the meaning of words he was sad if they knew the answer.
7 Taz deliberately asked Roger a word he would be unlikely to know.
8 Roger was delighted at being asked a question by Taz.
9 A leotard is an animal.
10 Roger woke Taz up because he wanted to tell him what he thought 'leotard' meant.

Reading comprehension: Unit 1

Vocabulary in context

Choose the definition which best fits these words or phrases as they are used in the text.

1 *ghost town* (line 3)
a) a town haunted by evil spirits
b) a trading station
c) a town that has lost its life
d) a new settlement in the desert

2 *outback* (lines 3, 9)
a) unpopulated parts
b) northern regions
c) mining area
d) suburban belt

3 *had it on his books* (line 6)
a) had read about it
b) had an official record of it
c) had the intention of writing about it
d) had a book about the town

4 *no-hoper* (line 8)
a) a man who has little chance of succeeding
b) a man who has had a lot of bad luck
c) a man who has just lost his job
d) a man who is seriously ill

5 *cast down* (line 20)
a) delighted
b) relieved
c) surprised
d) disappointed

6 *upset* (line 28)
a) displeased
b) amused
c) puzzled
d) grateful

Summary

Make a short summary of this story. Try to limit yourself to *two* sentences for each paragraph of the text.

Unit 2

The underworld

Let us take a brief look at the planet on which we live. As Earth hurtles through space at a speed of 70,000 miles an hour, it spins, as we all know, on its axis, which causes it to be flattened at the Poles. Thus if you were to stand at sea level at the North or South Pole you would be 13 miles nearer the centre of the earth than if you stood on the Equator.

The earth is made up of three major layers – a central core, probably metallic, some 4000 miles across, a surrounding layer of compressed rock, and to top it all a very thin skin of softer rock, only about 20 to 40 miles thick – that's about as thin as the skin of an apple, talking in relative terms.

The pressure on the central core is unimaginable. It has been calculated that at the centre it is 60 million pounds to the square inch, and this at a temperature of perhaps 10,000 degrees Fahrenheit. The earth's interior, therefore, would seem to be of liquid metal – and evidence for this is given by the behaviour of earthquakes.

When an earthquake occurs, shock waves radiate from the centre just as waves radiate outwards from the point where a stone drops into a pond. And these waves pulsate through the earth's various layers. Some waves descend vertically and pass right through the earth, providing evidence for the existence of the core and an indication that it is fluid rather than solid. Thus, with their sensitive instruments, the scientists who study earthquakes, the seismologists, can in effect X-ray the earth.

Northern India, and more especially that part of Northern Pakistan known as Baluchistan, is a particularly active seismic area. In Baluchistan one of the greatest earthquake disasters of modern times occurred, in 1935, when the town of Quetta was destroyed and 30,000 people lost their lives. Today, Quetta is the home of a geophysical observatory where scientists make a special study of earthquakes. One of the practical tasks of these seismologists in Quetta has been to calculate ways of making buildings safe against earthquake tremors, and nowadays all houses in the town are built according to seven approved designs. As a result, in a great earthquake near Quetta only a few years ago, practically all the buildings stood up and no lives were lost.

Iceland is one of the most active volcanic regions of the world. And it was to Iceland that Jules Verne sent the hero of his book *A Journey to the Centre of the Earth*. This intrepid explorer clambered down the opening of an extinct volcano and followed its windings until he reached the earth's core. There he found great oceans, and continents with vegetation. This conception of a hollow earth we now know to be false. In the 100 years since Jules Verne published his book, the science of vulcanology, as it is called, has made great strides. But even so the deepest man has yet penetrated is about 10,000 feet. This hole, the Robinson Deep mine in South Africa, barely scratches the surface; so great is the heat at 10,000 feet that were it not for an elaborate

air-conditioning system, the miners working there would be roasted. Oil borings   40
down to 20,000 feet have shown that the deeper they go, the hotter it becomes.

The temperature of the earth at the centre is estimated to be anything between 3,000 and 11,000 degrees Fahrenheit. Some scientists believe that this tremendous heat is caused by the breaking-down of radio-active elements, which release large amounts of energy and compensate for the loss of heat from the earth's surface. If this theory is   45
correct, then we are all living on top of a natural atomic powerhouse.
(By Radio UNESCO)

Multiple choice

Read the passage carefully, then answer the following questions.
Choose the response which best reflects the meaning of the text.

1 The outer layer of the Earth is compared to the skin of an apple because
a) it is only 20 to 40 miles thick.
b) it is thin in proportion to the Earth's mass.
c) it is relatively thin compared with the central core.
d) it is softer than the other layers.

2 Which of the following is *not* true?
   It is thought that the interior of the Earth is not solid because
a) there is great pressure at the centre.
b) earthquake waves can move vertically.
c) the outer layer is made of rock.
d) the heat at the centre is too great.

3 The Robinson Deep mine in South Africa is
a) too deep to work in.
b) too hot to work in.
c) still in use.
d) very close to the surface.

4 Since the publication of Jules Verne's book it has been proved that
a) the centre of the earth is not hollow.
b) oil borings cannot go deeper than 20,000 feet.
c) the earth is hot at the centre because heat is lost at the surface.
d) the earth is in danger of exploding.

True or false?

Without looking back at the text, decide whether the following statements
are true or false.
1 If you stand at the Equator you will be closer to the centre of the Earth than if you stand at the Poles.
2 The shock waves from an earthquake cannot pass through the Earth's central core.
3 Earthquakes often occur in Baluchistan.
4 All houses in Quetta are built according to the same design.
5 Jules Verne suggested that the Earth's centre was hollow.
6 The Earth is hottest at the surface.
7 It is not known exactly how hot it is at the centre of the Earth.

Reading comprehension: Unit 2

Vocabulary in context

Choose the definition which best fits these words or phrases as they are used in the text.

1 *axis* (line 2)
a) central line
b) side
c) orbit
d) gravitational pull

2 *major* (line 6)
a) large
b) important
c) main
d) distinct

3 *fluid* (line 18)
a) soft
b) liquid
c) thin
d) wet

4 *in effect* (line 19)
a) probably
b) effectively
c) actually
d) accurately

5 *a particularly active seismic area* (line 22) is one where
a) many seismologists work.
b) many people are killed.
c) many earthquakes occur.
d) many research centres have been built.

6 *intrepid* (line 33)
a) daring
b) foolish
c) experienced
d) curious

7 *extinct* (line 33)
a) unexplored
b) inactive
c) unsafe
d) inextinguishable

8 *has made great strides* (line 37)
a) caused a sensation
b) been accepted by scientists
c) developed immensely
d) improved mining techniques

8

Reading conprehension: Unit 2

9 *compensate for* (line 45)
a) prepare for
b) allow for
c) make up for
d) exchange for

Summary

Pick out the main point(s) from each paragraph and write a summary of the passage in not more than ten sentences.

Make use, if you like, of the following phrases:
– the Earth's slightly irregular shape
– immense pressure at the centre
– earthquake waves are not impeded by the central core
– houses in seismic regions must be specially designed
– Jules Verne was mistaken in thinking . . .
– heat increases with depth and this makes it impossible to . . .
– the Earth has its own internal supply of heat and energy.

Unit 3

When you have an accident

Drivers on the Basingstoke by-pass used to have their attention diverted by a sign that read – A MOMENT'S INATTENTION CAUSES ACCIDENTS. This self-defeating warning has now been removed, but its message is still very much to the point.

Almost anything can cause an accident. Apart from momentary inattention, it might be a minor miscalculation, a sudden fit of coughing, a bop on the head with a teddy-bear from a child in the back seat, an argument with the wife, fog, falling asleep at the wheel, bad eyesight, a glaring sun, ice, rain, wind, or snow – all these can make the difference between a tragic hit and a lucky miss.

Although human error plays its part, it is by no means the only cause of accidents. There must be some cause other than simple human error. Road construction plays its part: researchers have found that it is not at the obvious danger spots – sharp corners, cross-roads, narrow lanes – that accidents happen. It is on those roads where there are subtle visual traps, unexpected changes in the shape or surface of the road, or even insufficient or badly-placed signs. Wherever there is a 'black spot', it means that something is seriously wrong with the road. Why else did the careless driving of so many come out at that particular spot?

What the law requires when you have an accident

There are, firstly, the legal formalities of exchanging names and addresses with others involved in an accident and, in certain cases, informing the police. However, you are required by law to stop after an accident only if:
1 Somebody other than yourself in or outside your car has been injured.
2 A vehicle not your own has been damaged.
3 Any horse, cow, donkey, sheep, or dog has been injured.

It has been said that if a driver continues unaware of causing injury he must be acquitted. But the courts are wary of that excuse. Furthermore, the driver himself must wait at the scene; it is not enough for him to leave his chauffeur or a friend to attend to the boring formalities while he goes off on more important business.

If you have been involved in an accident and have stopped, you must give your name, address, and registration number to anyone who has a good reason for requesting it; this means anyone affected by the accident. If somebody is injured, the driver must produce his insurance certificate on request. If these formalities are complied with it is not necessary to wait for the arrival of the police. It is, however, often wise to do so. The police are expert at drawing plans, taking measurements and photographs and gathering other evidence. In your absence the police could be given a biased story against you; and you yourself might want to point out certain features of the accident to the police.
(From *The Sunday Times* Magazine)

Reading comprehension: Unit 3

Multiple choice

Read the passage carefully, then answer the following questions.
Choose the response which best reflects the meaning of the text.

1 'A MOMENT'S INATTENTION CAUSES ACCIDENTS' (line 2) is a self-defeating warning because
a) it is not true.
b) it will distract the driver's attention.
c) it is too difficult to understand.
d) it is too long to be read while driving a car.

2 '... *by no means* the only cause of accidents' (line 9), means
a) without doubt
b) in no way
c) probably not
d) surely not

3 'subtle visual traps' (line 13), are
a) places where the police hide in order to trap motorists.
b) parts of the road which are deceptive to the driver's eye.
c) danger spots such as sharp corners and cross-roads.
d) places where there are too many road-signs.

4 You must stop after an accident (line 19), if
a) you have been injured by somebody.
b) your car has been damaged.
c) you have injured somebody else.
d) you have witnessed the accident.

5 After an accident you should wait for the police because
a) it is against the law to drive off.
b) they have to examine your papers.
c) somebody may give them a false account of the accident.
d) they have to note the position of your car.

True or false?

Without looking back at the text, decide whether the following statements are true or false.

1 Drivers on the Basingstoke by-pass used to ignore the sign.
2 Road construction is not one of the major causes of accidents.
3 A 'black spot' is a part of the road where there are no signs.
4 You have to stop after an accident even if you are the only person who has been injured.
5 If a driver does not stop after an accident he cannot be taken to court.
6 After an accident you have to give your name to anyone who asks for it.
7 If you do not wait for the police after an accident they will make up a story against you.

Reading comprehension: Unit 3

Vocabulary in context

Choose the definition which best fits these words or phrases as they are used in the text.

1 *diverted* (line 1)
a) attracted
b) sharpened
c) improved
d) tested

2 *insufficient* (line 14)
a) too small
b) too few
c) too confusing
d) too old

3 *unaware* (line 23)
a) not conscious
b) not caring
c) not certain
d) not believing

4 *acquitted* (line 24)
a) arrested
b) fined
c) released
d) prosecuted

5 *wary* (line 24)
a) tired of
b) suspicious of
c) used to
d) ignorant of

6 *registration number* (line 28)
a) the number of your driving licence
b) the number of your insurance policy
c) the number of your car engine
d) the number of your car

7 *complied with* (line 30)
a) understood
b) observed
c) explained
d) forgotten

Unit 4

Detectives' lives – fact and fantasy

Real policemen, both in Britain and the United States, hardly recognise any resemblance between their lives and what they see on TV – if they ever get home in time. There are similarities, of course, but the cops don't think much of them.

The first difference is that a policeman's real life revolves round the law. Most of his training is in criminal law. He has to know exactly what actions are crimes and what evidence can be used to prove them in court. He has to know nearly as much law as a professional lawyer, and what is more, he has to apply it on his feet, in the dark and rain, running down an alley after someone he wants to talk to.

Little of his time is spent in chatting to scantily-clad ladies or in dramatic confrontations with desperate criminals. He will spend most of his working life typing millions of words on thousands of forms about hundreds of sad, unimportant people who are guilty – or not – of stupid, petty crimes.

Most television crime drama is about *finding* the criminal: as soon as he's arrested, the story is over. In real life, finding criminals is seldom much of a problem. Except in very serious cases like murders and terrorist attacks – where failure to produce results reflects on the standing of the police – little effort is spent on searching. The police have an elaborate machinery which eventually shows up most wanted men.

Having made an arrest, a detective really starts to work. He has to prove his case in court and to do that he often has to gather a lot of different evidence. Much of this has to be given by people who don't want to get involved in a court case. So, as well as being overworked, a detective has to be out at all hours of the day and night interviewing his witnesses and persuading them, usually against their own best interests, to help him.

A third big difference between the drama detective and the real one is the unpleasant moral twilight in which the real one lives. Detectives are subject to two opposing pressures: first, as members of a police force they always have to behave with absolute legality; secondly, as expensive public servants they have to get results. They can hardly ever do both. Most of the time some of them have to break the rules in small ways.

If the detective has to deceive the world, the world often deceives him. Hardly anyone he meets tells him the truth. And this separation the detective feels between himself and the rest of the world is deepened by the simple-mindedness – as he sees it – of citizens, social workers, doctors, law-makers, and judges, who, instead of stamping out crime punish the criminals less severely in the hope that this will make them reform. The result, detectives feel, is that nine-tenths of their work is re-catching people who should have stayed behind bars. This makes them rather cynical.
(From an article by Peter Laurie in the *TV Times*)

Reading comprehension: Unit 4

Multiple choice

Read the passage carefully, then answer the following questions.
Choose the response which best reflects the meaning of the text.

1 It is essential for a policeman to be trained in criminal law
a) so that he can catch criminals in the streets.
b) because many of the criminals he has to catch are dangerous.
c) so that he can justify his arrests in court.
d) because he has to know nearly as much about law as a professional lawyer.

2 The everyday life of a policeman or detective is
a) exciting and glamorous.
b) full of danger.
c) devoted mostly to routine matters.
d) wasted on unimportant matters.

3 When murders and terrorist attacks occur the police
a) prefer to wait for the criminal to give himself away.
b) spend a lot of effort on trying to track down their man.
c) try to make a quick arrest in order to keep up their reputation.
d) usually fail to produce results.

4 The real detective lives in 'an unpleasant moral twilight' (line 25) because
a) he is an expensive public servant.
b) he must always behave with absolute legality.
c) he is obliged to break the law in order to preserve it.
d) he feels himself to be cut off from the rest of the world.

5 Detectives are rather cynical because
a) nine-tenths of their work involves arresting people.
b) hardly anyone tells them the truth.
c) society does not punish criminals severely enough.
d) too many criminals escape from jail.

True or false?

Without looking back at the text, decide whether the following statements are true or false.

1 Policemen feel that the image of their lives shown on TV is not accurate.
2 A policeman does not need any special training in law.
3 Policemen and detectives spend a great deal of time at the typewriter.
4 Television crime plays tend to concentrate on the search for the criminal.
5 In real life, finding criminals is one of the policeman's greatest problems.
6 The detective's work is over once the arrest has been made.
7 People are usually willing to give evidence.
8 Detectives are not permitted to break the law.
9 Most detectives feel that criminals are punished too severely.
10 Much of the detective's work involves arresting former **criminals**.

Reading comprehension: Unit 4

Vocabulary in context

Choose the definition which best fits these words or phrases as they are used in the text.

1 *don't think much of them* (line 3)
a) don't like them
b) don't give them much thought
c) don't consider them accurate
d) don't care about them at all

2 *and what is more* (line 7)
a) nevertheless
b) even worse
c) besides
d) after all

3 *reflects on the standing of the police* (line 16)
a) has an effect on the influence of the police
b) is harmful for the reputation of the police
c) shows up the inadequacy of the police
d) makes the police work even harder

4 *most wanted men* (line 17)
a) the most dangerous criminals
b) most people the police are looking for
c) the men the police are most interested in arresting
d) most of the dangerous criminals

5 *usually against their own best interests* (line 22)
a) although they are usually not interested (in helping him)
b) although it is not usually to their own advantage (to help him)
c) although it usually goes against their personal wishes (to help him)
d) although they usually know that they are unable (to help him)

6 *as he sees it* (line 32)
a) because he is aware of it
b) in his opinion
c) as he imagines it
d) since he knows about it

Summary and discussion

In this passage the author speaks of the differences between real detectives and TV detectives. Most of the typical features of the TV detective, however, are implied not stated.
   First make a summary of the passage (one sentence for each paragraph), then make a list of the statements that are made about the life of the detective or policeman, e.g. that he is overworked.
   This list will be used for discussion after the listening comprehension passage has been worked through.

Unit 5

Oil wealth flows up the Voe

The newly signed £19.25m agreement between Shetland County Council and three major oil companies was celebrated with cups of tea served by helpful members of Lerwick's Women's Institute. It was not that the County Council did not want to entertain their gift-bearing guests, who had just handed over a cheque for £500,000 as first payment of a multi-million pound 'sweetener'. They would have liked to have served a splendid banquet, or even cocktails, but local catering firms, whose staff have gone away to better-paid jobs in oil-related industries, just could not cope. If the oil bosses noticed this particular labour shortage that they have helped to cause, they did not let on.

When this archipelago of Britain's 100 most northerly islands – as far away from London as Corsica – first realised it was close to the new massive oilfields, what it did was bold and shrewd. Shetland simply 'nationalised' oil development by obtaining legislation which would give her the power of compulsory purchase of any land which would be needed by oil companies, and the right to assume port and harbour authority powers.

Basic to the agreement between the County Council and oil companies, and to the promise of a specified revenue tied to the amount of oil brought ashore, is the establishment of a giant oil complex and pipeline terminal on the shores of bleak Sullom Voe.

Sullom Voe is now certain to become, within the next ten years, Britain's largest oil port and terminal. There are proposals for a tanker terminal, oil storage, gas separation and oil refinery plant, an oil-fired power station, and even rig and platform fabrication yards, together with a service base and repair yard.

Sullom Voe seemed to meet all the oilmen's requirements. It was a tried and proven deep-water anchorage and shelter, it was close to the oilfields, it was remote and relatively unpopulated.

Ian Clark, Shetland's county clerk – who has come to show that he is a match for any high-powered oilmen – has said that it was open to any other operators of pipelines to Sullom Voe to join the oil committee. He also emphasises that the offer of the £20m sweetener from the companies did not commit the council in any way and gave the oil firms no rights in connection with the Sullom complex.

With a rush now on to better-paid jobs with oil companies, local employers are already facing problems. Milk deliveries in Lerwick have stopped altogether – the milkman found his £32 a week job less attractive than one in oil and has departed. A shoeshop has closed because its staff left, one of the town's three bakeries has closed and another threatens to shut up the ovens. The newly-opened *Georges*, a long awaited good-food restaurant, has closed down again because it could not keep its staff. And now one of the town's dentists has shut up his surgery and become a North Sea diver.
(From an article in *The Sunday Times*)

Reading comprehension: Unit 5

Multiple choice

Read the passage carefully, then answer the following questions.
Choose the response which best reflects the meaning of the text.

1 The County Council did not give the oil companies' representatives a big reception because
a) they were too mean.
b) they did not want to entertain them.
c) they could not find a caterer.
d) they wanted to oblige the Women's Institute.

2 Sullom Voe is
a) a port.
b) a bay.
c) a town.
d) an oil-field.

3 Which of the following was *not* a reason for Sullom Voe being chosen by the oil companies?
a) It had very few inhabitants.
b) It had a tanker terminal.
c) It was near the oilfields.
d) It was a sheltered place.

4 The oil companies have paid £20 million to the County Council. In return for this
a) they have obtained exclusive rights to Sullom Voe.
b) the Council has given up its rights.
c) they will be allowed to build an oil terminal.
d) they will not be allowed to do anything.

5 Local employers in Lerwick are worried because
a) there is an unemployment crisis.
b) their employees are demanding higher wages.
c) people are leaving their jobs to go and work for the oil companies.
d) the oil companies are forcing people to leave their jobs.

True or false?

Without looking back at the text, decide whether the following statements are true or false.

1 Because of the oil boom there is a shortage of jobs on Shetland.
2 The oil companies have agreed to build a big oil complex.
3 Sullom Voe now belongs to the oil companies.
4 Only four oil companies will be allowed to use Sullom Voe.
5 Ian Clark has made a good bargain.
6 The oil companies have agreed to pay the Council a fixed sum for every barrel of oil brought ashore.

Reading comprehension: Unit 5

Vocabulary in context

Choose the definition which best fits these words or phrases as they are used in the text.

1 *sweetener* (lines 5, 30)
a) money for buying cakes and tea
b) money paid for oil
c) money paid for goodwill
d) money to buy land

2 *cope* (line 7)
a) stay
b) manage
c) leave
d) help

3 *let on* (line 9)
a) allow
b) reveal
c) complain
d) assist

4 *shrewd* (line 12)
a) difficult
b) brave
c) cunning
d) necessary

5 *tried and proven* (line 24)
a) well-planned
b) special
c) reliable
d) constantly used

6 *a match for* (line 27)
a) fiercely opposed to
b) not so good as
c) the equal of
d) determined to compete against

7 *Remote*
There is a phrase in paragraph 2 which means the same as this word. Which is it?

8 *Compulsory*
Which of these verbs is related in meaning?
a) may
b) must
c) could
d) should

18

Reading comprehension: Unit 5

9 *Specified revenue* refers to
a) a type of equipment
b) a form of legislation
c) a number of ships
d) a sum of money

10 *Bleak*
Which of these words does *not* go with 'bleak?'
a) bare
b) gay
c) cold
d) dreary

11 *Anchorage*
Does it help you to understand this word if you know that this is an anchor?

Summary

Make a summary of the passage in not more than *six* sentences. Remember that only really important information should be included in a summary.
Here are some guide-lines:
 – Because of labour shortage . . .
 – The oil companies have promised . . . and . . .
 – Shetland County Council 'nationalised' . . . when . . .
 – Sullom Voe . . .
 – The oilmen were looking for . . .
 – The fact that . . . does not mean . . .

Unit 6

Eyeless sight

When the first white men arrived in Samoa, they found blind men, who could see well enough to describe things in detail just by holding their hands over objects. In France just after the First World War, Jules Romain tested hundreds of blind people and found a few who could tell the difference between light and dark. He narrowed their photosensitivity down to areas on the nose or in the fingertips. In Italy the neurologist Cesare Lombroso discovered a blind girl who could 'see' with the tip of her nose and the lobe of her left ear. When a bright light was shone unexpectedly on her, she winced. In 1956 a blind schoolboy in Scotland was taught to differentiate between coloured lights and learned to pick out bright objects several feet away. In 1960 a medical board examined a girl in Virginia and found that, even with thick bandages over her eyes, she was able to distinguish different colours and read short sections of large print. The phenomenon is obviously not new, but it has reached new peaks of sensitivity in a young woman from a mountain village in the Urals.

    Rosa Kuleshova can see with her fingers. She is not blind, but because she grew up in a family of blind people, she learned to read Braille to help them and then went on to teach herself to do other things with her hands. In 1962 her physician took her to Moscow, where she was examined by the Soviet Academy of Science, and emerged a celebrity, certified as genuine. The neurologist Shaefer made an intensive study with her and found that, securely blindfolded with only her arms stuck through a screen, she could differentiate among three primary colours. To test the possibility that the cards reflected heat differently, he heated some and cooled others without affecting her response to them. He also found that she could read newsprint and sheet music under glass, so texture was giving her no clues. Tested by the psychologist Novomeisky, she was able to identify the colour and shape of patches of light projected on to her palm or on to a screen. In rigidly controlled tests, with a blindfold and a screen and a piece of card around her neck so wide that she could not see round it, Rosa read the small print in a newspaper with her elbow. And, in the most convincing demonstration of all, she repeated these things with someone standing behind her pressing hard on her eyeballs. Nobody can cheat under this pressure; it is even difficult to see clearly for minutes after it is released.

(From *Supernature* by Lyall Watson)

Multiple choice

Read the passage carefully, then answer the following questions.
Choose the response which best reflects the meaning of the text.

1 The first white men to visit Samoa found men who
a) were not entirely blind.

Reading comprehension: Unit 6

b) described things by touching them.
c) could see with their hands.
d) could see when they held hands.

2 What is the main idea of the first paragraph?
a) Very few people have the sensitivity of the blind.
b) Blind people can manage to see things, but only vaguely.
c) The eyes are not the only way of seeing.
d) It is possible to localise the photosensitive areas of the body.

3 Why did Shaefer put the paper under glass?
a) To make things as difficult as possible.
b) To stop the reflection of heat.
c) To prevent Rosa from feeling the print.
d) To stop her from cheating.

4 What was the most difficult test of her ability?
a) To read through glass, blindfolded.
b) To identify the colour and shape of light on a screen while securely blindfolded.
c) To carry out tasks with someone pressing on her eyeballs.
d) To work from behind a screen, blindfolded and with a card round her neck.

True or false?

Without looking back at the text, decide whether the following statements are true or false.

1 The men in Samoa were not quite blind.
2 Jules Romain found a lot of blind people who could see with their noses and ears.
3 The Italian girl enjoyed it when the light was shone on her ear.
4 A girl called Virginia could read newsprint even when she was blindfolded.
5 Rosa Kuleshova lives on a mountain peak.
6 Her family taught her everything about seeing with her fingers.
7 Shaefer found that temperature did not affect her ability to differentiate between colours.
8 Her ability to read with her fingers did not depend on the feel of the print.
9 Rosa's ability to see was confined to her fingers.
10 It is impossible to doubt the results of the last test.

Vocabulary in context

1 *Patches* (line 24) are
a) rays
b) waves
c) spots
d) lines

2 Many parts of the body are mentioned in the passage. How many of them can you identify on this diagram?

3 Find a synonym for 'pick out' in the first paragraph.

4 Find a single word in paragraph 2 which means the same as 'thick bandages over her eyes'.

5 Someone has committed a murder. Here are the suspects:
 – Jim Peters, slim, 6 feet tall, 20 years old
 – Mary Peters, fat, 4 feet tall, 50 years old
 – John Perkins, slim, 5 feet tall, 25 years old
 – Michael Rogers, slim, 6 feet tall, 65 years old
 – Peter Jones, fat, 6 feet tall, 18 years old
    Someone saw the murderer. Now you *narrow down* the suspects. We know:
 – it was a man (this *eliminates* Mary)
 – he was tall (this eliminates John)
 – he was slim (etc.)
 – he was young (etc.)

Reading comprehension: Unit 6

6 Can you *pick out* the man with a moustache in this picture?

7 Which of these pictures shows a peak?

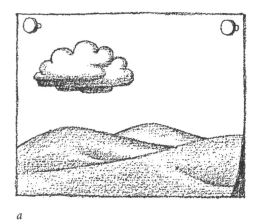
a

b

8 *Texture*
   The texture of silk is smooth
   The texture of granite is . . .?

Reading comprehension: Unit 6

9 Which of these men is *cheating*?

Unit 7

Gold

Mankind's fascination with gold is as old as civilisation itself. The ancient Egyptians esteemed gold, which had religious significance to them, and King Tutankhamun was buried in a solid-gold coffin 3300 years ago. The wandering Israelites worshipped a golden calf, and the legendary King Midas asked that everything he touched be turned into gold.

Not only is gold beautiful, but it is virtually indestructible. It will not rust or corrode; gold coins and products fabricated from the metal have survived undamaged for centuries. Gold is extremely easy to work with; one ounce, which is about the size of a cube of sugar, can be beaten into a sheet nearly 100 square feet in size, and becomes so thin that light passes through it. An ounce of gold can also be stretched into a wire 50 miles long. Gold conducts electricity better than any other substance except copper and silver, and it is particularly important in the modern electronics industry.

People have always longed to possess gold. Unfortunately, this longing has also brought out the worst in the human character. The Spanish *conquistadores* robbed palaces, temples, and graves, and killed thousands of Indians in their ruthless search for gold. Often the only rule in young California during the days of the gold rush was exercised by the mob with a rope. Even today, the economic running of South Africa's gold mines depends largely on the employment of black labourers who are paid about £40 a month, plus room and board, and who must work in conditions that can only be described as cruel. About 400 miners are killed in mine accidents in South Africa each year, or one for every two tons of gold produced.

Much of gold's value lies in its scarcity. Only about 80,000 tons have been mined in the history of the world. All of it could be stored in a vault 60 feet square, or a supertanker.

Great Britain was the first country to adopt the gold standard, when the Master of the Mint, Sir Isaac Newton, established a fixed price for gold in 1717. But until the big discoveries of gold in the last half of the nineteenth century – starting in California in 1848 and later in Australia and South Africa – there simply wasn't enough gold around for all the trading nations to link their currencies to the precious metal.

An out-of-work prospector named George Harrison launched South Africa into the gold age in 1886 when he discovered the metal on a farm near what is now Johannesburg. Harrison was given a £12 reward by the farmer. He then disappeared and reportedly was eaten by a lion.

One of the big gold-mining areas in the Soviet Union is the Kolyma River region, once infamous for its prison camp. The camp has gone, but in a way nothing has changed. Many ex-prisoners have stayed on to work the mines and are supervised by ex-guards.

Despite the current rush to buy gold, 75 per cent of the metal goes into jewellery.

Reading comprehension: Unit 7

Italy is the biggest user of gold for this purpose, and many Italian jewellers even tear   40
up their wooden floors and burn them to recover the tiny flecks of gold.

   Historically, the desire to hoard gold at home has been primarily an occupation of the working and peasant classes, who have no faith in paper money. George Bernard Shaw defended their instincts eloquently: 'You have to choose between trusting to the   45
natural stability of gold and the natural stability of the honesty and intelligence of the members of the government', he said, 'and with due respect to these gentlemen, I advise you . . . to vote for gold.'
(From an article in *Newsweek*)

Multiple choice

Read the passage carefully, then answer the following questions.
Choose the response which best reflects the meaning of the text.

1 One of the disadvantages of gold is that
a) it loses its shape too easily.
b) it is easy to destroy.
c) it is expensive to mine.
d) it is of no use in industry.

2 Gold has always been considered a precious metal because
a) money is made of it.
b) it is rare.
c) a small quantity goes a long way.
d) it has religious significance.

3 During the days of the gold-rush in California
a) people had to mark out their gold claims with rope.
b) people carried rope instead of guns.
c) hanging was a common form of punishment.
d) rope was the symbol of law and order.

4 After the big gold discoveries in the late nineteenth century
a) most nations adopted the gold standard.
b) the trading nations were unable to get enough gold.
c) gold coins were used by most nations.
d) gold ceased to be an important metal.

5 The gold standard is
a) the average price of gold on the world market.
b) a basis for determining the value of currency.
c) the amount of gold required by a nation before its currency can be made convertible.
d) a means of determining the quality of gold.

6 George Bernard Shaw thought that
a) the members of the government were honest and intelligent.
b) the value of gold was likely to change unexpectedly.
c) one could place more faith in gold than in politicians.
d) gold was more valuable than paper money.

Reading comprehension: Unit 7

True or false?

Without looking back at the text, decide whether the following statements are true or false.

1 Gold was of no use to the Egyptians.
2 It is extremely difficult to destroy gold.
3 Gold is a poor conductor of electricity.
4 Gold mining is dangerous.
5 Before the big gold discoveries in the nineteenth century nobody was interested in gold.
6 Harrison made a fortune from his discovery of gold.
7 Most gold today is used for jewellery.
8 Italy is the greatest consumer of gold in the world.
9 Peasants and workers used to keep gold at home because they did not trust paper money.
10 Bernard Shaw thinks it is better to rely on politicians than on gold.

Vocabulary in context

Choose the definition which best fits these words or phrases as they are used in the text.

1 *esteemed* (line 2)
a) valued
b) worshipped
c) produced
d) needed

2 *not only is gold beautiful* (line 6)
a) gold is not beautiful . . .
b) gold is both beautiful and . . .
c) gold is only beautiful, and not . . .
d) gold is beautiful, but . . .

3 *virtually indestructible* (line 6)
a) has the virtue of being easy to destroy
b) is almost impossible to destroy
c) can be easily extracted
d) is extremely difficult to break

4 *corrode* (line 7)
a) be eaten away
b) melt
c) change colour
d) lose shape

5 *ruthless* (line 16)
a) hopeless
b) needless
c) heartless
d) useless

Reading comprehension: Unit 7

6 *there simply wasn't enough gold around* (line 29)
a) the gold mines were exhausted
b) gold was being stored by the wealthy nations
c) gold was difficult to find
d) there was too little gold available

7 *current* (line 39)
a) continuous
b) present
c) recent
d) periodic

8 *for this purpose* (line 40)
a) for this reason
b) for buying gold
c) for trading purposes
d) for making jewellery

9 *stability* (line 45)
a) constancy
b) value
c) function
d) scarcity

Unit 8

Flicker

Walter examined hundreds of people who had never had any kind of fit or attack and found that about one in every twenty responded to carefully adjusted flicker. They experienced 'strange feelings' or faintness or swimming in the head; some became unconscious for a few moments or their limbs jerked in rhythm with the light. As soon as any such sensation was reported, the flicker was turned off to prevent a complete convulsion. In other subjects, the flicker had to be exactly matched with the brain rhythm to produce any effects. A feedback circuit, in which the flashing light was actually fired by the brain signals themselves, produced immediate epileptic seizures in more than half the people tested.

Driving down a tree-lined avenue with the sun flickering through the trunks at a certain rhythm can be very disturbing. There is a record of a cyclist who passed out on several occasions while travelling home down such an avenue. In his case the momentary unconsciousness stopped him from pedalling, so he slowed down to a speed at which the flicker no longer affected him and came round in time to save himself from falling. But a motor-car has more momentum, and the chances are that it would keep going at the critical speed and influence the driver long enough to make him lose control altogether. There is no way of knowing how many fatal crashes have occurred in this way.

In another case, a man found that every time he went to the cinema he would suddenly find that he was consumed by an overwhelming desire to strangle the person sitting next to him. On one occasion he even came to his senses to discover that he had his hands clutched around his neighbour's throat. When he was tested, it was found that he developed violent limb jerking when the flicker was set at twenty-four cycles per second, which is exactly the rhythm of film recorded at twenty-four frames a second.

The implications of this discovery are enormous. Every day we are exposed to flicker in some way and run the risk of illness or fatal fits. The flash rate of fluorescent lights at 100 to 120 per second is too high for convulsions, but who knows what effect it may be having on those exposed to it for many hours each day?
(From *Supernature* by Lyall Watson)

Multiple choice

Read the passage carefully, then answer the following questions.
Choose the response which best reflects the meaning of the text.
1 Walter was interested in the reactions of
a) epileptics.
b) cyclists.
c) normal people.
d) motorists.

Reading comprehension: Unit 8

2 When the experiment was going on and it was noticed that people began to have strange feelings
a) the experiment was stopped.
b) the flicker was matched with their brain rhythm.
c) a feedback circuit was used.
d) they were allowed to have an epileptic fit.

3 Flicker is likely to affect car drivers more than cyclists because
a) cyclists can close their eyes for a few seconds.
b) cars cannot slow down in time.
c) the rhythm of flicker is faster for cyclists.
d) cyclists cannot go fast enough to be affected.

4 The man in the cinema wanted to strangle his neighbour because
a) the film was very violent.
b) he did not like his neighbour.
c) he responded to the flicker of the film.
d) he was mentally unsound.

5 The author is worried about the effects of light because
a) fluorescent lights can produce fits.
b) we are all exposed to too much flicker.
c) we may be affected by flicker without realising it.
d) the flash rate of fluorescent lights is too high.

True or false?

Without looking back at the text, decide whether the following statements are true or false.

1 Walter examined people who were subject to fits.
2 When they began to have a convulsion he stopped the experiment.
3 Most people do not respond to flashing lights.
4 The cyclist fell off his bicycle.
5 Drivers are affected very suddenly by flicker.
6 The man went to the cinema because he enjoyed strangling people.
7 The man in the cinema was influenced by the speed of flicker of the film.
8 Fluorescent lighting causes people to have fits.

Vocabulary in context

Choose the definition which best fits these words or phrases as they are used in the text.

1 *flicker* (lines 2, 5, 6, 14, 22, 26)
a) bright light
b) fluorescent light
c) flashing light
d) sunlight

Reading comprehension: Unit 8

2 *limb* (line 22)
a) eye or ear
b) arm or leg
c) foot or hand
d) hair or skin

3 *seizure* (line 8)
a) a fit
b) a feeling
c) a rhythm
d) a signal

4 *fired* (line 8)
a) burnt up
b) knocked out
c) set off
d) held up

5 *passed out* (line 11)
a) went faster
b) lost consciousness
c) fell off
d) fell asleep

6 *came round* (line 14)
a) regained consciousness
b) changed direction
c) turned quickly
d) looked back

7 *momentum* (line 15)
a) the faster something is going the more difficult it is to stop
b) the heavier something is the more difficult it is to stop

8 *overwhelming* (line 19)
a) insane
b) inexplicable
c) irresponsible
d) irresistible

Unit 9

Shaka – King of the Zulus

Shaka's military career started at about the same time as Napoleon's came to an end at Waterloo. Neither man had ever heard of the other, yet they had a surprising amount in common, particularly in their genius for war and politics. Had Shaka been born in Europe he too might well have altered the course of world affairs. As it was, he built the Zulu nation. And he would have destroyed it had it not been for the courage of a minor chieftain named Gala.

When he was still only twenty-nine, Shaka seized the throne of the Zulus. It took him very little time to turn the Zulu people into a first-class fighting race because he was absolutely ruthless, never moving without an escort of 'slayers', whose job it was to kill anyone who displeased him in any way. If his warriors could not run 50 miles a day, they died; if they were unable to dance barefoot on a carpet of jungle thorns, they died; if they showed anything less than suicidal courage in battle, they would be unhesitatingly murdered by the slayers. Shaka was inhuman, perhaps, but he built up a formidable army in a very short time.

Shaka had already increased his kingdom from 100 square miles to 100,000 when personal tragedy struck: his mother, Nandi, died. Nandi was the one person for whom Shaka felt deep affection, and on her death something seemed to snap in his mind. What followed was unbelievable, but it was recorded by an Englishman named Flynn who was in the area at the time.

Nandi was buried, and 12,000 warriors were ordered to guard her grave for a year. Then Shaka sent his *impis* or regiments to scour the countryside and punish all those who had failed to be present at the funeral. Only after this had been done did he announce his orders for mourning: no crops were to be planted the following year; no milk was to be used – it was to be drawn from the cow and poured on to the earth; and all women who were found with child during the following year were to be put to death with their husbands. As the staple diet of the Zulus consisted of grain and milk products, this order was little less than a sentence of national starvation.

Shaka now developed a brooding and bitter spirit: 'I have conquered the world but lost my mother', he would cry, 'and all taste has gone out of my life.'

After two months of intensive mourning over Nandi's death, the country was in a desperate state. The fields were overgrown with weeds and one of the staple diets, namely milk, was no longer on the food list. Total ruin now faced the Zulu nation, and it was obvious that those who had not been killed by Shaka would certainly starve to death.

Finally, one of Shaka's warriors, Gala, determined to end the tyranny. 'It is enough', he told his family. 'Someone must tell the Great Elephant. I shall do it.' Gala's family stared at him in horror: to challenge the King's wishes at such a moment was to ask for instant death. But Gala took his warrior's stick and went to Bulawayo to see Shaka. When he reached the right distance from the royal enclosure he shouted: 'O King, you have destroyed your country. What will you reign over? Will you create a new race? Shall we all die because your mother died? You have destroyed the country. Your country will be inhabited by other kings, for your people will die of hunger. As for me, O King, I say you are dead yourself through this mother of yours. Stuff a stone into your stomach. This is not the first time anyone has died in Zululand!'

Stuff a stone into your stomach! This was the Zulu way of saying: 'pull yourself together'. There was a gasp of horror from the onlookers, and the slayers took a grip on their clubs. That a man should dare to speak to the King in such a way was unthinkable, and Gala's life seemed to be measured in seconds. But Shaka turned to his Councillors and said: 'What use are you to me? You never dared, like Gala, to tell me to stuff a stone in my stomach. Now let all men know that crops are to be planted as usual and that milk may be drunk again. And as for you', said Shaka turning to Gala, 'you shall have a mighty gift of many cattle.'
(From an article in *Look and Learn*)

Multiple choice

Read the passage carefully, then answer the following questions.
Choose the response which best reflects the meaning of the text.

1 '... *had it not been for* the courage of a minor chieftain ...' (line 5) means
a) thanks to
b) in spite of
c) but for
d) because of

2 Shaka was inhuman because
a) he made himself King of the Zulus.
b) he gave special privileges to his bodyguard.
c) he set standards he could not keep himself.
d) he had no respect for human life.

3 '... all those *who had failed to be present* at the funeral' (line 22) means
a) all who had not come
b) all who had not been able to come
c) all who had not brought presents
d) all who had not announced their arrival to Shaka

4 Shaka's orders were 'little less than a sentence of national starvation' (line 27) because
a) the Zulus were too lazy to cultivate anything but grain.
b) the Zulus were already on a diet.
c) the Zulus' food consisted mainly of grain and milk products.
d) the Zulus had nothing else to eat.

5 '... to challenge the King's wishes at such a moment was *to ask for instant death*' (line 38) means
a) to want to die at once
b) to beg to be killed at once
c) to run the risk of being killed on the spot
d) to ask for a quick and painless death

Reading comprehension: Unit 9

6 Gala told Shaka to 'stuff a stone into his stomach' (line 44) because
a) he wanted to prove his courage to his family.
b) he thought Shaka was only pretending to mourn his mother's death.
c) he thought Shaka's grief was exaggerated.
d) he wanted to gain favour with Shaka.

True or false?

Without looking back at the text, decide whether the following statements are true or false.

1 Napoleon and Shaka were contemporaries.
2 Shaka was elected King of the Zulus before he was thirty.
3 Shaka's soldiers were extremely fit.
4 Shaka's 'slayers' performed the function of a bodyguard.
5 The Zulu people did not obey Shaka's mourning orders.
6 Gala was disrespectful to Shaka.
7 Shaka was not angry with Gala after he had spoken.

Vocabulary in context

Choose the definition which best fits these words or phrases as they are used in the text.

1 *as it was* (line 4)
a) it seemed
b) it is said
c) all the same
d) for this reason

2 *ruthless* (line 9)
a) fearless
b) heartless
c) careless
d) senseless

3 *formidable* (line 14)
a) enormous
b) impressive
c) well-trained
d) famous

4 *scour* (line 21)
a) burn
b) search
c) patrol
d) destroy

5 *staple diet* (lines 26, 31)
a) favourite food
b) special diet
c) main source of income
d) basic food

Unit 10

Packaging: the insane waste of making things to be thrown away

To get a chocolate out of a box requires a considerable amount of unpacking: the box has to be taken out of the paper bag in which it arrived; the cellophane* wrapper has to be torn off, the lid opened and the paper removed; the chocolate itself then has to be unwrapped from its own piece of paper. But this insane amount of wrapping is not confined to luxuries. It is now becoming increasingly difficult to buy anything that is not done up in cellophane, polythene, or paper.

The package itself is of no interest to the shopper, who usually throws it away immediately. Useless wrapping accounts for much of the refuse put out by the average London household each week. So why is it done? Some of it, like the cellophane on meat, is necessary, but most of the rest is simply competitive selling. This is absurd. Packaging is using up scarce energy and resources and messing up the environment.

Little research is being carried out on the costs of alternative types of packaging. Just how possible is it, for instance, for local authorities to salvage paper, pulp it, and recycle it as egg-boxes? Would it be cheaper to plant another forest? Paper is the material most used for packaging – 20 million paper bags are apparently used in Great Britain each day – but very little is salvaged.

A machine has been developed that pulps paper then processes it into packaging, e.g. egg-boxes and cartons. This could be easily adapted for local authority use. It would mean that people would have to separate their refuse into paper and non-paper, with a different dustbin for each. Paper is, in fact, probably the material that can be most easily recycled; and now, with massive increases in paper prices, the time has come at which collection by local authorities could be profitable.

Recycling of this kind is already happening with milk bottles, which are returned to the dairies, washed out, and refilled. But both glass and paper are being threatened by the growing use of plastic. More and more dairies are experimenting with plastic bottles, and it has been estimated that if all the milk bottles necessary were made of plastic, then British dairies would be producing the equivalent of enough plastic tubing to encircle the earth every five or six days!

The trouble with plastic is that it does not rot. Some environmentalists argue that the only solution to the problem of ever growing mounds of plastic containers is to do away with plastic altogether in the shops, a suggestion unacceptable to many manufacturers who say there is no alternative to their handy plastic packs.

It is evident that more research is needed into the recovery and re-use of various

---

* *cellophane*: a thin, colourless, material, useful for keeping products clean and dry. It serves as the outer wrapping for many things, such as cigarette-packs, chocolate-boxes, packs of razor-blades, playing-cards, greetings-cards, etc.

materials and into the cost of collecting and recycling containers as opposed to producing new ones. Unnecessary packaging, intended to be used just once, and making things look better so more people will buy them, is clearly becoming increasingly absurd. But it is not so much a question of doing away with packaging as using it sensibly. What is needed now is a more sophisticated approach to using scarce resources for what is, after all, a relatively unimportant function.
(From an article in *The Times*)

Multiple choice

Read the passage carefully, then answer the following questions.
Choose the response which best reflects the meaning of the text.

1 'This insane amount of wrapping is not confined to luxuries' (line 1), means
a) not enough wrapping is used for luxuries.
b) more wrapping is used for luxuries than for ordinary products.
c) it is not only for luxury products that too much wrapping is used.
d) the wrapping used for luxury products is unnecessary.

2 The 'local authorities' are
a) the Town Council.
b) the police.
c) the paper manufacturers.
d) the most influential citizens.

3 If paper is to be recycled
a) more forests will have to be planted.
b) the use of paper bags will have to be restricted.
c) people will have to use different dustbins for their rubbish.
d) the local authorities will have to reduce the price of paper.

4 British dairies are
a) producing enough plastic tubing to go round the world in less than a week.
b) giving up the use of glass bottles.
c) increasing the production of plastic bottles.
d) re-using their old glass bottles.

5 The environmentalists think that
a) more plastic packaging should be used.
b) plastic is the most convenient form of packaging.
c) too much plastic is wasted.
d) shops should stop using plastic containers.

6 The author thinks that
a) the function of packaging is not important.
b) people will soon stop using packaging altogether.
c) not enough research has been done into the possibilities of recycling.
d) the cost of recycling is so great that it is better to produce new materials than use old ones.

Reading comprehension: Unit 10

True or false?

Without looking back at the text, decide whether the following statements are true or false.

1 Too many products nowadays are wrapped in unnecessary packaging.
2 Most London families refuse to throw away packaging.
3 The countryside is being spoilt by the overproduction of packaging.
4 It is possible to use paper again.
5 Most of the 20 million paper bags used each day are recovered and re-used.
6 The rising price of paper will make it worthwhile for local authorities to collect waste-paper.
7 There is no danger that plastic will ever replace glass and paper.
8 Many dairies are using plastic bottles in their laboratories.
9 Plastic is difficult to destroy.
10 People are beginning to ask if packaging should not be done away with altogether.

Vocabulary in context

Choose the definition which best fits these words or phrases as they are used in the text.

1 *confined* (line 5)
a) used for
b) restricted to
c) needed for
d) suited to

2 *accounts for* (line 8)
a) makes up
b) compensates for
c) is recovered from
d) is kept out of

3 *So why is it done?* (line 9)
a) Why do people buy things they don't need?
b) Why is so much wrapping thrown away?
c) Why do the shops try to sell things people don't want?
d) Why is so much unnecessary wrapping used?

4 *most of the rest* (line 10)
a) the other kinds of packaging
b) what is left over
c) the other shopkeepers
d) the rest of the time

5 *messing up* (line 11)
a) spoiling
b) altering
c) improving
d) poisoning

6 *apparently* (line 15)
a) obviously
b) regularly
c) undoubtedly
d) supposedly

7 *recycled* (line 21)
a) reduced
b) reproduced
c) re-used
d) retailed

8 *some environmentalists argue* (line 29)
a) some environmentalists disagree
b) some environmentalists claim
c) some environmentalists fear
d) some environmentalists admit

9 *handy* (line 32)
a) attractive
b) easy to hold
c) convenient
d) easy to destroy

10 *as opposed to* (line 34)
a) instead of
b) in order to
c) as well as
d) in spite of

Summary

Many different points are made in this passage. Try to summarise each paragraph in *two* sentences, and give a short heading (such as one finds in newspaper articles) to convey the main point of each section.

Unit 11

How lions hunt

Male lions are rather reticent about expending their energy in hunting – more than three-quarters of kills are made by lionesses. Setting off at dusk on a hunt, the lionesses are in front, tensely scanning ahead, the cubs lag playfully behind, and the males bring up the rear, walking slowly, their massive heads nodding with each step as if they were bored with the whole matter. But slothfulness may have survival value. With lionesses busy hunting, the males function as guards for the cubs, protecting them particularly from hyenas.

Hunting lionesses have learnt to take advantage of their environment. Darkness provides them with cover, and at dusk they often wait near animals they want to kill until their outlines blend into the surroundings. Small prey, such as gazelle, present lions with no problem. They are simply grabbed with the paws, or slapped down and finished off with a bite in the neck. A different technique is used with large animals, such as wildebeest. Usually a lioness pulls her prey down after running up behind it, and then seizes it by the throat, strangling it. Or she may place her mouth over the muzzle of a downed animal, and suffocate it.

Lions practise remarkably sophisticated cooperative hunting techniques. Sighting prey, lionesses usually fan out and stalk closer until one is within striking distance. The startled herd may scatter or bolt to one side right into a hidden lioness. Sometimes lionesses surround their quarry. While perhaps three crouch and wait, a fourth may backtrack and then circle far around and approach from the opposite side, a technique not unknown in human warfare.

No obvious signals pass between the lions, other than that they watch one another. A tactic may also be adapted to a particular situation. One pride of lions often pursued prey at the end of a narrow strip of land between two streams. Several lionesses would sit and wait until gazelle wandered into this natural dead-end. Then they would spread out and advance quite in the open, having learnt that the gazelle would not try to escape by running into the bush beside the river, but would run back the way they had come.

A lioness has no trouble pulling down an animal of twice her weight. But a buffalo, which may scale a ton, presents problems. One lioness and a young bull battled for an hour and a half, the buffalo whirling around to face the cat with lowered horns whenever she came close. Finally she gave up and allowed him to walk away. But on another occasion, five males came across an old bull. He stood in a swamp, belly-deep in mud and water, safely facing his tormentors on the shore. Suddenly, inexplicably, he plodded towards them, intent it seemed on committing suicide. One lion grabbed his rump, another placed his paws on the bull's back and bit into the flesh. Slowly, without trying to defend himself, the buffalo sank to his knees and, with one lion holding his throat and another his muzzle, died of suffocation.

(From *Serengeti, a Kingdom of Predators* by George Schaller)

Reading comprehension: Unit 11

Multiple choice

Read the passage carefully, then answer the following questions. Choose the response which best reflects the meaning of the text.

1 When lions hunt the females go in front because
a) they have to look after the cubs.
b) the males are not strong enough to kill.
c) they can see better than the males at dusk.
d) most of the killing is done by lionesses.

2 Male lions are
a) too lazy to hunt.
b) not interested in hunting.
c) unwilling to waste their strength.
d) interested only in killing hyaenas.

3 Which of the following is *not* true?
a) Lions are difficult to see in the evening.
b) The hunting techniques of lions are also used in warfare.
c) Lions can kill animals twice their own size.
d) Lions always use the same techniques when hunting.

4 The old bull buffalo was killed because
a) he was trying to commit suicide.
b) he left the swamp.
c) there were five lions against him.
d) he was too old to fight.

True or false?

Without looking back at the text, decide whether the following statements are true or false.

1 The cubs are guarded by their mothers.
2 A lion will never attack an animal larger than itself.
3 Lions cannot hunt in the evening because their eyesight is poor.
4 Lions are unable to communicate with one another.
5 Buffaloes are frightened of lions.
6 Lions prefer to hunt alone.

Vocabulary in context

Choose the definition which best fits these words or phrases as they are used in the text.

1 *reticent* (line 1)
a) uncertain
b) unhappy
c) reluctant
d) lazy

Reading comprehension: Unit 11

2 *scanning ahead* (line 3)
a) running in front
b) sniffing at the air
c) observing the terrain
d) waiting for the males

3 *sighting prey* (lines 16–17)
a) while hunting for their prey
b) when they are sighted by their prey
c) having spotted their prey
d) in order to catch sight of their prey

4 *adapted (to)* (line 23)
a) changed to suit
b) adopted for
c) employed in
d) worked out for

5 *inexplicably* (line 34)
a) unexpectedly
b) without any hesitation
c) uncertainly
d) for no clear reason

Unit 12

Uri Geller's extraordinary powers

Uri Geller is said to have superhuman powers. Scientists, however, are still not able to decide whether he is a genius or a charlatan – or both. This article describes some of the experiments he agreed to do at the Stanford Research Institute.

Uri first did five tests of telepathy using either numbers or drawings. He was correct in four out of five tries. He then asked to be given some metal objects. Dr Puthoff took out a copper ring, a fork, and his silver chain, which Uri briefly touched. Dr Puthoff put his hand over these objects. Uri placed his hand over Dr Puthoff's hand. After Uri had concentrated for some 30 seconds on the objects, Dr Puthoff removed his hand. The copper ring had gone from a circle to an egg-shape. The scientists were all amazed.

Next came work in the laboratory. Uri's first test was with an instrument called a magnetometer, which measures the strength of magnetic fields. Uri concentrated hard on the instrument and finally the needle deflected, indicating that his mind had simulated the effect that a magnetic field would produce. The test was repeated many times and each time it was observed that Uri's mind had a visible effect on the needle. Nevertheless, he had to make an immense effort to simulate this 'mental magnetic field'.

The next day an attempt was made to see if the change in shape of the metal ring could be recorded in some way. One of the scientists held a metal ring under water. Uri touched this ring with one finger. The entire procedure was recorded by sound waves which made a picture similar to an X-ray, showing the bones of the hands and the metal ring. This sound picture was then passed on to a television screen and videotaped.

While Uri was concentrating it was noticed that the television picture and the videotape recording were affected. In addition, it was seen that the brass ring was being flattened by Uri's mind power. The experiment lasted for several hours and during this time the scientists working on the floor below Uri experienced considerable difficulty with their computers, one of which could not be used at all while he was concentrating.

The experiments went on for five weeks. Among the most interesting of the laboratory tests was one designed to show Uri Geller's power of 'seeing' shapes and figures drawn by perfect strangers and placed in sealed envelopes. At no time during the experiment did Geller have any advance knowledge of the target material. He admitted that he could not get about one in five of the drawings, but he succeeded in reproducing 80 per cent of the drawings correctly. He would look at the envelope, which he did not touch, chat for several minutes and then draw his representation of it. Very often the sketch he made was identical in size to the drawing inside the envelope.

In another experiment a single dice was placed in a metal box and shaken. Geller was then asked to guess which number was showing on top of the dice. Out of ten tries he twice refused to guess. The other eight times he got the correct number. Statistically, this is a probability of about a million to one!

The conclusion of the Stanford Research Institute is that the experiments were well controlled and, although they should not be interpreted as proof of psychic functioning, they offer sufficient proof of the phenomena to deserve further study.

(From an article in the *Daily Mail*)

Multiple choice

Read the passage carefully, then answer the following questions.
Choose the response which best reflects the meaning of the text.

1 Uri Geller
a) broke Dr Puthoff's ring.
b) turned the ring into an egg.
c) bent the ring in his hands.
d) changed the shape of the ring without touching it.

2 Uri Geller
a) was able to measure the strength of magnetic fields.
b) was able to simulate a magnetic field without any difficulty.
c) was interested in testing the strength of the magnetometer.
d) had great difficulty in deflecting the needle of the magnetometer.

3 The scientists wanted to
a) have tangible proof of the effects of Geller's 'mind power'.
b) see if Geller could disturb the functioning of a computer.
c) take an X-ray of Geller's hand.
d) prove that Geller could not change the shape of metal without touching it.

4 Geller's reproductions of the drawings in the envelopes were
a) identical in every way.
b) occasionally similar.
c) correct in shape but not in size.
d) correct in shape and often in size as well.

5 The experiment with the dice showed that Geller was
a) good at guessing.
b) good at arithmetic.
c) gifted with unusual psychic powers.
d) a charlatan.

True or false?

Without looking back at the text, decide whether the following statements are true or false.

1 Uri was not allowed to touch Dr Puthoff's ring before the experiment began.
2 After less than a minute's concentration, Uri succeeded in changing the shape of the ring.

Reading comprehension: Unit 12

3 The scientists were deeply impressed by Uri's performance.
4 A magnetometer is a machine for magnetising metal.
5 Uri had no difficulty in simulating the mental magnetic field.
6 Uri was able to change the shape of the metal ring by the power of his concentration.
7 Uri was not able to reproduce any of the drawings placed in sealed envelopes.
8 In the experiment with the dice Uri's guesses were all correct.
9 The Stanford Research Institute considers that the experiments with Uri were a failure.

Vocabulary in context

Choose the definition which best fits these words or phrases as they are used in the text.

1 *amazed* (line 7)
a) amused
b) suspicious
c) astonished
d) unimpressed

2 *hard* (line 9)
a) close to
b) a little
c) intensely
d) with difficulty

3 *simulate* (line 11)
a) to excite
b) to copy
c) to affect
d) to destroy

4 *perfect* (line 28)
a) complete
b) kind
c) intelligent
d) important

5 *would look* (line 31)
a) insisted on looking
b) always looked
c) asked if he might look
d) was obliged to look

Reading comprehension Unit 12:

6 Which of the following represents a *dice*?

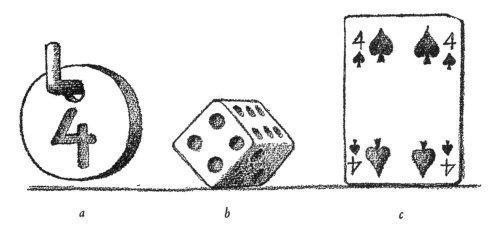

      a   *b*   *c*

7 *interpreted* (line 37)
a) accepted
b) considered
c) offered
d) rejected

Unit 13

Battery buses

A battery-driven bus, which is not only quiet and pollution-free but competitive with the conventional bus on cost and performance, has been developed by a group of British companies.

The prototype, a fifty-passenger single-deck vehicle, is to go into operation in Manchester shortly, and discussions with the Department of the Environment are expected to lead to a further batch of twenty going into regular passenger service in Manchester within two years, and possibly in other cities, including London.

Unlike the small government-sponsored battery bus now undergoing trials in provincial cities, whose low speed and range effectively limits it to city-centre operation, the new Silent Rider, with a range of 40 miles between charges and a speed of 40 m.p.h., will take its place with diesel buses for normal urban and suburban services.

Its capital cost is higher (about £20,000 compared with £13,500) but lower maintenance and fuel costs bring it down to a fully competitive cost with the diesel bus over a thirteen-year life, without taking into account the environmental benefits. The Chloride battery group, which is developing it in partnership with SELNEC (South-East Lancashire and North-East Cheshire Passenger Transport Authority) is confident of a market potential of 400 vehicles a year by 1980.

The prototype weighs 16 tons, of which the batteries and passengers account for 4 each. It has a single set of batteries, which take three and a half hours to recharge, against the normal eight hours of passenger traffic.

A larger, Mark II version is being designed with two sets of batteries which can be changed in under a minute. That will allow low-cost night charging and greater operational flexibility.

(From an article in *The Times*)

Multiple choice

Read the passage carefully, then answer the following questions.
Choose the response which best reflects the meaning of the text.
1 What had been the main factor preventing the development of battery buses?
a) Their limited range.
b) Their high cost.
c) Their heavy weight.
d) Their loud noise.

2 Battery buses have some advantages over conventional buses. Which of these advantages is not mentioned in the text?
a) They use less fuel.

Reading comprehension: Unit 13

b) They make less noise.
c) They produce less pollution.
d) They cost less to produce.

3 The Mark II model will have a number of advantages over the prototype. Which of these is *not* one of them?
a) It will carry more passengers.
b) It will have a wider range.
c) It can be used all through the day.
d) It will cost less to recharge.

4 How many of the new Silent Riders are in regular service at the moment?
a) none
b) twenty
c) one
d) fifty

5 Why will battery buses cost less than conventional buses in the long run?
a) They will spread the capital cost over a long period.
b) They will be stronger and last longer.
c) They will use less fuel and cost less to maintain.
d) They will be charged at night when electricity costs less.

True or false?

Without looking back at the text, decide whether the following statements are true or false.
 1 Battery buses are more expensive to run than conventional ones.
 2 There are twenty battery buses in service at the moment.
 3 There is only one type of battery bus in existence.
 4 The Silent Rider is a government-sponsored project.
 5 The Silent Rider will be able to operate only in city centres.
 6 Eventually it will cost about the same as conventional buses.
 7 Within a few years the makers hope to sell 400 a year.
 8 The prototype is smaller than the Mark II version.
 9 It will be possible to use the Mark II version at any time of day.
 10 The Mark II takes three and a half hours to recharge.

Vocabulary in context

Choose the definition which best fits these words or phrases as they are used in the text.
1 *conventional* (line 2)
a) cheap
b) normal
c) special
d) city

2 *prototype* (lines 4, 19)
a) earliest model
b) projected model
c) latest model
d) approved model

47

Reading comprehension: Unit 13

3 *range* (lines 9, 10)
a) distance from one point to another
b) equal distance from a fixed point in any direction
c) speed over a fixed distance
d) distance round the edge of a circle

4 *suburban services* (line 12)
a) services which serve city centres
b) services which serve country areas
c) services which serve provincial towns
d) services which serve areas around cities

5 *a market potential of 400 vehicles a year* (line 18)
a) the certainty of selling 400 a year
b) the necessity of selling 400 a year
c) the possibility of selling 400 a year
d) the desirability of selling 400 a year

Summary

Make a summary of the main points of the passage in not more than *six* sentences.

Unit 14

Shape and waves

The idea of shape having an influence on the functions taking place within it is not a new one. A French firm once produced a special container for making yogurt, because that particular shape enhanced the action of the micro-organism involved in the process. The brewers of a Czechoslovakian beer tried to change from round to angular barrels but found that this resulted in a deterioration in the quality of their beer despite the fact that the method of processing remained unchanged. A German researcher has shown that mice with identical wounds heal more quickly if they are kept in spherical cages. Architects in Canada report a sudden improvement in schizophrenic patients living in trapezoidal hospital wards.

It is possible that all shapes have their own qualities and that the forms we see around us are the result of combinations of environmental frequencies. In the eighteenth century the German physicist Ernst Chladni discovered a way of making vibration patterns visible. He fixed a thin metal plate on to a violin, scattered sand on the plate, and found that when a bow was drawn across the strings, the sand arranged itself into beautiful patterns. These arrangements, now known as Chladni's figures, have been extensively used in physics to demonstrate wave function, but they also show very well that different frequencies produce patterns with different forms. By juggling around with powders of different densities and by playing notes with a wide range of frequencies, it is possible to induce a pattern to take on almost any form. It is interesting, and perhaps significant, that Chladni's figures most often resemble forms found in nature. Concentric circles, such as the annual rings in a tree trunk; alternating lines, such as the stripes on a zebra's back; hexagonal grids, such as the cells in a honeycomb; radiating wheel spokes, such as the canals in a jellyfish; vanishing spirals, such as those of shellfish – all these commonly occur. The study of this phenomenon, the effect of waves on matter, is called cymatics.

The basic principle of cymatics is that environmental pressures are brought to bear in wave patterns and that matter responds to these pressures by taking a form that depends on the frequency of the waves. There are a limited number of frequencies involved, and nature tends to respond to these in predictable ways, by repeating a number of limited functional forms. The corkscrew pattern of an updraught of heated air is mirrored in the growth of a creeper twined around a tree and in the arrangement of the atoms in a molecule of DNA. The manta ray flows through tropical waters with muscular waves that run in lines across its broad, flat back like wind-blown patterns on the surface of the sea. Given the same problem, nature will usually find the same solution. It could not do this with such widely differing raw materials unless they were responding to identical pressures.

(From *Supernature* by Lyall Watson)

Reading comprehension: Unit 14

Multiple choice

Read the passage carefully, then answer the following questions.
Choose the response which best reflects the meaning of the text.

1 The main idea of the first paragraph is that
a) we need to be careful before choosing the shape of any container.
b) round or spherical shapes are preferable in the food industry.
c) the shape of an object affects what happens inside it.
d) the main applications of shape are in the food industry and in medicine.

2 The main idea in the second paragraph is that
a) all shapes have their own special qualities.
b) Chladni's figures demonstrate the function of waves.
c) a change in frequency of vibration changes the shape of patterns.
d) geometric patterns are extremely common in nature.

3 Cymatics is the study of
a) the shapes found in nature.
b) the effect waves have on things.
c) the frequency of waves.
d) the effect of shape on function.

4 The main idea of the third paragraph is that
a) there is only a limited number of shapes in nature.
b) the shape of a thing depends on wave frequency.
c) there are not many wave frequencies, therefore not many shapes in nature.
d) the environmental pressures brought to bear on matter are identical.

5 Nature tends to produce a limited range of shapes because
a) the materials it uses are very similar.
b) the influences exerted on matter are similar.
c) different densities combine with different frequencies.
d) there is only a limited number of forms which are functional.

True or false?

Without looking back at the text, decide whether the following statements are true or false.

1 The shape of an object has no effect on what happens inside it.
2 The beer from angular barrels tasted better.
3 Mental patients get better in wards which have a special shape.
4 It has been proved that all shapes have special properties.
5 Ernst Chladni was a Czech violinist.
6 When the frequency of vibration changes, the pattern also changes.
7 Chladni's figures often take on most unusual forms.
8 The same limited range of shapes is repeated in nature.
9 The manta ray causes the patterns on the surface of the sea.
10 Very different substances produce the same shape when they are exposed to the same influences.

Reading comprehension: Unit 14

Vocabulary in context

1 *... resulted in a deterioration ...* (line 5)
Find a word in the first paragraph which means the opposite of this phrase.

2 *... identical ...* (lines 7, 36)
Find a word in the passage which means the same as this. Then find *two* words which mean the opposite.

3 Which of the following series of numbers is most *predictable*?
a) 1, 3, 5, 7, 9, 11, 13, 15 ...
b) 5, 17, 56, 100, 103 ...
c) 10, 25, 50, 95, 100 ...

4 Which of the following shapes is *angular*?

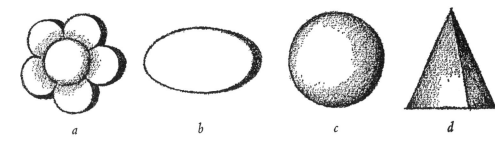

a *b* *c* *d*

5 *juggling around with* (lines 17–18) means
a) throwing into the air
b) trying out different arrangements
c) playing different tunes
d) making different patterns

6 *induce* (line 19) means
a) force
b) produce
c) invent
d) persuade

7 *frequency* (line 28)
Which of these wave patterns has the highest (i.e. *greatest*) frequency?

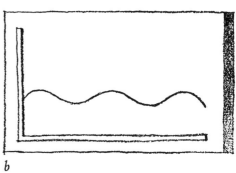
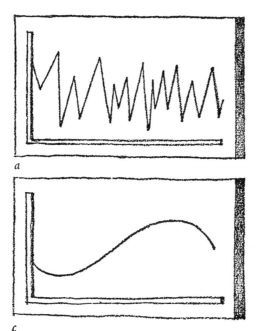

8 *scattered* (line 13) means
a) dropped vertically
b) threw anyhow
c) arranged carefully
d) spread sideways

9 Which of these two sets of influences represents *environmental* pressures?
a) weather conditions   b) a headache
   altitude   blood pressure
   radiation from the sun   rheumatism
   noise from cars   body temperature
   atmospheric pollution   clothing

Reading comprehension: Unit 14

10 In which picture is the line *z twined around* the tree?

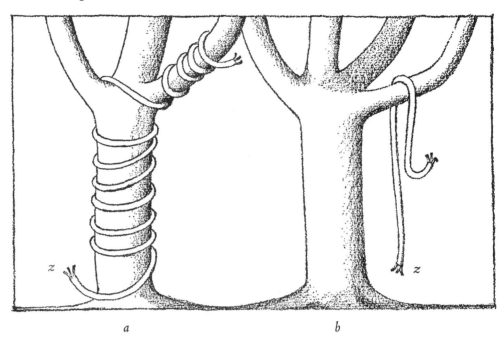

11 Find the words or phrases in the passage which correspond to the following shapes:

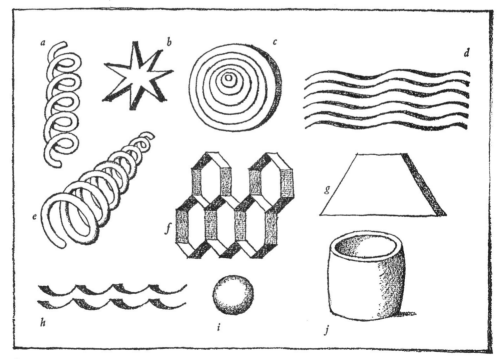

Summary

Write a summary of the passage in not more than *five* sentences.

Unit 15

Lost world of the Kalahari

We were trying to stalk a dazzle of zebras which flashed in and out of a long strip of green and yellow fever trees, with an ostrich, its feathers flared like a ballet skirt around its dancing legs, on their flank, when suddenly two shots, fired quickly one after the other, snapped the tense silence ahead.

My blood went cold within me. Instinctively I looked at Samutchoso. His face was without expression and yet I knew he had heard and that a change accordingly had taken place within him. With an acute sense of guilt, I realised I had forgotten to keep my promise to him. My anxieties in the swamp, my absorption with the problem of Spode, the long journey out and back from Johannesburg, and many other things had overlaid the moment when he and I had first discussed the journey to the hills. I had completely overlooked the essential condition of the promise extracted by him from me: that there should be no killing on our way to the hills. I had forgotten to tell our companions of Samutchoso's account of the spirits' law against killing on approach to their home.

John and Jeremiah were close by the Land-Rover disembowelling a wart-hog. Vyan was followed by Cheruyiot with a steenbuck across his shoulders. The expression on Samutcho's face was almost more than I could bear.

From there we pushed on faster because the passage over the blackened plain was easy. By eleven o'clock the highest of the hills rose above the blue of distance. After so many weeks in flat land and level swamp the sudden lift of the remote hills produced an immediate emotion and one experienced immediately that urge to devotion which once made hills and mountains sacred to man who then believed that wherever the earth soared upwards to meet the sky one was in the presence of an act of the spirit as much as a feature of geology. I thought of the psalmist's: 'I will uplift my eyes unto the hills from whence cometh my help', and marvelled that the same instinct had conducted Samutchoso to the hills to pray.

The nearer we came the stronger this impression grew, and as the hills rose at last clear above the bush they seemed to communicate their own atmosphere to us all. The highest could not have been more than a thousand feet. But they rose sheer out of the flat plain and were from the base up made entirely of stone, and this alone, in a world of deep sand, gave them a sense of mystery. The others, too, felt it.

The sun was setting by the time we had made camp, collected wood for our fires and installed ourselves for a stay of several days. Still no sound or movement came from bush or hills. Even a stir of evening air would have been welcome to ease the immovable and shining heat hanging in the horseshoe bowl of rocks. Just before dark I took my gun and walked alone to the narrow gap between the highest of the hills in the hope that there I might meet some cooling air. But it was just as bad there so I started back at a quickened pace because the light was fast beginning to fail, and the silent raised rock faces made me feel acutely uncomfortable. In that red afterglow of an immense

Reading comprehension: Unit 15

Kalahari sunset they had a strange, living personality as if their life had been only temporarily suspended, and they might wake up, at any moment step down, and walk the desert. 40

At this point I was deeply startled by a sound coming from the rocks on my right. I swung round, my gun ready, and the hair slowly creeping at the back of my neck.
(From *Lost World of the Kalahari* by Laurens van der Post)

Multiple choice

Read the passage carefully, then answer the following questions.
Choose the response which best reflects the meaning of the text.

1 When the shots were fired, Samutchoso
a) did not hear them.
b) felt very guilty.
c) showed no feelings.
d) looked angry.

2 The author had made a promise to Samutchoso
a) a long time before.
b) that morning.
c) in Johannesburg.
d) the moment before.

3 The author's companions killed the animals because
a) they had ignored his warning.
b) he had ordered them to.
c) they needed food for the evening.
d) he had forgotten to warn them.

4 They felt a strong sensation when they first saw the hills because
a) the hills were sacred to them.
b) they were frightened by them.
c) the hills were a contrast to the plains.
d) they believed in spirits.

5 The hills were mysterious because they were
a) very high.
b) made of steep rock.
c) sacred to them.
d) completely windless.

6 How long did the group intend to stay in the hills?
a) until morning
b) a few weeks
c) one day
d) a few days

7 Why did the author go for a walk in the hills?
a) Because he was feeling hot.
b) Because he wanted to see the sunset.

Reading comprehension: Unit 15

c) Because he wanted to hunt.
d) Because he hoped to meet someone.

8 Why did he turn back?
a) Because it got cold suddenly.
b) Because he saw some strange faces.
c) Because a noise frightened him.
d) Because the atmosphere made him uneasy.

True or false?

Without looking back at the text, decide whether the following statements are true or false.

  1 The writer shot at the zebra.
  2 He knew that Samutchoso had heard the shot because his face changed.
  3 He had promised that no one should kill anything on the way to the hills.
  4 Samutchoso did not believe in spirits.
  5 The writer had told his friends about his promise to Samutchoso.
  6 They were all deeply impressed by the hills.
  7 At one time people believed that hills were the homes of the gods.
  8 The hills were very high.
  9 The hills were made of sand.
10 It was already dark when they put up their tents.
11 It was windy in the gap between the hills.
12 The writer came down from the gap between the hills because he felt uneasy.
13 The writer was frightened by the sound from behind the rock.

Vocabulary in context

Choose the definition which best fits these words or phrases as they are used in the text.
1 *stalk* (line 1)
a) shoot
b) photograph
c) follow
d) catch

2 *flared* (line 2)
a) on fire
b) hanging down
c) spread out
d) going up and down

3 *on their flank* (line 3)
a) behind them
b) in front of them
c) beside them
d) between them

4 *Instinctively I looked at Samutchoso* (line 5)
a) I looked because my instincts told me he had heard.
b) I looked because that is the sort of thing I often do.

c) I looked before I had time to think what I was doing.
d) I looked before he had time to change his expression.

5 *absorption with* (line 8)
a) forgetting of
b) solution of
c) irritation over
d) concentration on

6 *soared* (line 23)
a) fell
b) hurt
c) rose
d) exploded

7 *sheer* (line 29)
a) steeply
b) quickly
c) roughly
d) gently

8 *suspended* (line 41)
a) ended
b) interrupted
c) changed
d) delayed

Summary

Make a summary of the passage in not more than *eight* sentences.

Unit 16

Population growth and industry

We have looked at some of the ways in which biological factors affect human population growth. However, although biological laws underlie all the phenomena of population, once societies reach an advanced level of technology and culture it is more meaningful to explain what is happening in terms of sociological, economic and political influences.

The study of population statistics in themselves is called 'demography'. All advanced countries now collect detailed statistics on births, marriages and deaths, and every few years a census of the population is taken. In England these figures are published by the General Register Office in London. World figures for population changes are much more difficult to compile because many underdeveloped countries do not keep complete records. However, a very detailed list of the available statistics is published every year in the United Nations Demographic Yearbook.

From a careful study of these figures, demographers have worked out a description of what they think happened in the history of the population of a modern industrial nation. Throughout most of human history, they believe, man has had a very high death-rate and a high birth-rate. The death-rate may have been due to infanticide, epidemic disease or starvation, but it was typical of traditional tribal and peasant societies. Since it was balanced by large numbers of births, the size of the population remained stable. Modern populations in Africa, and much of South America and Asia, are examples of what may have been universal in the past. In these countries, a very large proportion of the population belongs to an age-group capable of becoming parents. This means that, compared with modern industrial countries, the birth-rate will be very high, not only because women have bigger families, but because the proportion of women capable of having children is also much higher.

This is a stage of high potential growth because, if the death-rate could be reduced, the population would increase very rapidly. In about one-fifth of the world, modern medicine has reduced the death-rate and here the population explosion is greatest. South-eastern Europe, some South American countries and India are all more or less at this stage. It seems almost certain that many more countries will arrive at this situation by the end of the century. The available statistics suggest that the modern industrial nations of the West passed through a phase like this in the nineteenth century.

After this transitional growth stage, a third change took place in the Western nations. The birth-rate began to drop, and by the 1930s several North European countries had reached a new stable level with low birth-rates combined with low death-rates. In some countries the population declined, and governments actively encouraged people to have more children.

The three stages in this transition can be summarised in a graph. Each has a distinctive economic arrangement. In the earliest phase there is a very low level of productivity, energy sources are primitive, and the standard of living is very low. At the middle stage, agriculture becomes more productive but does not always keep up with population growth, and industrial growth begins. The third stage has a very high standard of living, great efficiency and universal, sophisticated technology.

This 'transition' theory of population growth is based on what happened in modern industrial nations. If the theory is applicable to the underdeveloped countries, we would expect that if they industrialise and modernise there will be a decline in fertility until the population is stabilised. If industrialisation is not achieved in the next one hundred years there are two other possibilities for slowing the growth of the population. The death-rate could begin to rise again because medicine and hygiene cannot keep up with the continued rise in population. Alternatively, there could be a decline in fertility before industrialisation. This has never happened before, but it is just possible that a peasant population might be influenced by a widespread birth-control campaign if they had enough help and encouragement from the government.
(From *Human Populations* by David Hay)

Multiple choice

Read the passage carefully, then answer the following questions.
Choose the response which best reflects the meaning of the text.

1 Full details of births, marriages and deaths are recorded
a) by the United Nations Demographic Yearbook.
b) by most underdeveloped countries.
c) by all fully developed countries.
d) by the General Register office only.

2 In past centuries
a) birth rates were high and death rates were low.
b) birth rates were low and so were death rates.
c) birth rates were low and death rates were high.
d) birth rates were high and so were death rates.

3 In the nineteenth century the population in the West
a) began to drop.
b) suddenly increased.
c) was stabilised.
d) began to fluctuate.

4 The economic conditions in a country with a low birth-rate and a low death-rate would be
a) low standards of living and no industry.
b) productive agriculture and a little industry.
c) low standards of living and efficient agriculture.
d) high standards of living and very efficient industry.

5 The passage mentions several ways in which population growth might be controlled. Which of the following is not one of these ways?
a) industrialisation and a higher standard of living
b) an increase in the death-rate
c) an increase in health and hygiene
d) birth control programmes

Reading comprehension: Unit 16

True or false?

Without looking back at the text, decide whether the following statements are true or false.

1. In advanced societies biological factors offer the best explanation of population phenomena.
2. The study of population statistics is called demagogy.
3. Only advanced countries keep full population statistics.
4. The United Nations Demographic Yearbook is the best place to look for population statistics.
5. Demographers know exactly what happened in the population history of advanced countries.
6. In the past, populations were stable.
7. The proportion of women able to have children is larger in industrial countries.
8. Modern medicine has produced a great increase in the population of a third of the world.
9. In the 1930s some European countries started a widespread birth control campaign.
10. Industrialisation and modernisation will certainly take place in the underdeveloped countries.

Vocabulary in context

1 '... all countries now collect detailed statistics on births, marriages, and deaths' (line 7)
What is the one word from the passage which describes this collection of statistics?

2 *compile* (line 10) means
a) find out
b) draw up
c) check up
d) send out

3 Which of these two graphs shows a *stable population*?

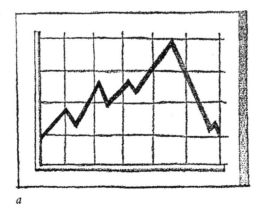 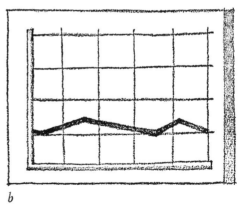

a   b

4 *potential* (line 25) refers to something which
a) has happened
b) is happening
c) could happen
d) must happen

60

Summary

Pick out the main points from each paragraph and write a summary of the passage in not more than *eleven* sentences. Use these suggestions if you wish:
- Although . . .
- Whereas all advanced . . . many underdeveloped . . . but the United Nations . . .
- Demographers believe that throughout . . . but because . . . population was stable.
- This is . . . because . . . and in fact this has happened . . . and will probably . . . century.
- Following this, . . .
- Each of these three stages . . .
- A stage of . . . is followed by . . . which finally results in . . .
- If this theory of what happened . . . can be applied . . . then . . .
- If not then either . . . or . . .
- Although . . . it is just possible . . .

Unit 17

Our first words

Is language, like food, a basic human need without which a child at a critical period of life can be starved and damaged? Judging from the drastic experiment of Frederick II in the thirteenth century it may be. Hoping to discover what language a child would speak if he heard no mother tongue he told the nurses to keep silent.

All the infants died before the first year. But clearly there was more than language deprivation here. What was missing was good mothering. Without good mothering, in the first year of life especially, the capacity to survive is seriously affected.

Today no such drastic deprivation exists as that ordered by Frederick. Nevertheless, some children are still backward in speaking. Most often the reason for this is that the mother is insensitive to the cues and signals of the infant, whose brain is programmed to mop up language rapidly. There are critical times, it seems, when children learn more readily. If these sensitive periods are neglected, the ideal time for acquiring skills passes and they might never be learned so easily again. A bird learns to sing and to fly rapidly at the right time, but the process is slow and hard once the critical stage has passed.

Linguists suggest that speech milestones are reached in a fixed sequence and at a constant age, but there are cases where speech has started late in a child who eventually turns out to be of high IQ (Intelligence Quotient). At twelve weeks a baby smiles and utters vowel-like sounds; at twelve months he can speak simple words and understand simple commands; at eighteen months he has a vocabulary of three to fifty words. At three he knows about 1000 words which he can put into sentences, and at four his language differs from that of his parents in style rather than grammar.

Recent evidence suggests that an infant is born with the capacity to speak. What is special about Man's brain, compared with that of the monkey, is the complex system which enables a child to connect the sight and feel of, say, a teddy-bear with the sound pattern 'teddy-bear'. And even more incredible is the young brain's ability to pick out an order in language from the hubbub of sound around him, to analyse, to combine and recombine the parts of a language in novel ways.

But speech has to be triggered, and this depends on interaction between the mother and the child, where the mother recognises the cues and signals in the child's babbling, clinging, grasping, crying, smiling, and responds to them. Insensitivity of the mother to these signals dulls the interaction because the child gets discouraged and sends out only the obvious signals. Sensitivity to the child's non-verbal cues is essential to the growth and development of language.

(From an article in *The Observer*)

Multiple choice

Read the passage carefully, then answer the following questions.
Choose the response which best reflects the meaning of the text.

Reading comprehension: Unit 17

1 Frederick II's experiment was 'drastic' because
a) he wanted to prove that children are born with the ability to speak.
b) he ignored the importance of mothering to the infant.
c) he was unkind to the nurses.
d) he wanted to see if the children would die before they reached the age of one.

2 The reason some children are backward in speaking today is that
a) they do not listen carefully to their mothers.
b) their brains have to absorb too much language at once.
c) their mothers do not respond to their attempts to speak.
d) their mothers are not intelligent enough to help them.

3 By 'critical times' (line 11) the author means
a) difficult periods in the child's life.
b) moments when the child becomes critical towards its mother.
c) important stages in the child's development.
d) times when mothers often neglect their children.

4 Which of the following is *not* implied in the passage?
a) The faculty of speech is inborn in man.
b) Children do not need to be encouraged to speak.
c) The child's brain is highly selective.
d) Most children learn their language in definite stages.

5 If the mother does not respond to her child's signals
a) the child will never be able to speak properly.
b) the child will stop giving out signals.
c) the child will invent a language of its own.
d) the child will make little effort to speak.

True or false?

Without looking back at the text, decide whether the following statements are true or false.

1 Frederick II lived more than 500 years ago.
2 Frederick's experiment proved that children are born with the ability to speak.
3 Good mothering is important only after the child has learned to speak.
4 Children are slow to begin speaking if their mothers do not respond to the noises they make.
5 By the age of a year and a half the child's vocabulary is still under 100 words.
6 By the age of four children still make many grammatical mistakes.
7 The author does not believe that children select and analyse their language.

Vocabulary in context

Choose the definition which best fits these words or phrases as they are used in the text.

1 *deprivation* (lines 6, 8)
a) inability
b) removal
c) need
d) disturbance

2 *survive* (line 7)
a) learn
b) live
c) communicate
d) overcome

3 *backward* (line 9)
a) inaccurate
b) shy
c) undeveloped
d) slow

4 *mop up* (line 11)
a) absorb
b) analyse
c) understand
d) develop

5 *readily* (line 12)
a) slowly
b) by reading
c) easily
d) systematically

Unit 18

A sunrise on the veld

(While walking in the bush early one morning, a young boy comes across a wounded buck being eaten to death by ants.)

He ran closer, and again stood still, stopped by a new fear. Around him the grass was whispering and alive. He looked wildly about, then down. The ground was black with ants, great energetic ants that took no notice of him, but hurried and scurried towards the fighting shape, like glistening black water flowing through the grass.

And, as he drew in his breath and pity and terror seized him, the beast fell and the screaming stopped. Now he could hear nothing but one bird singing, and the sound of the rustling whispering ants.

He peered over at the writhing blackness that jerked convulsively with the jerking nerves. It grew quieter. There were small twitches from the mass that still looked vaguely like the shape of a small animal.

It came into his mind that he could shoot it and end its pain; and he raised the gun. Then he lowered it again. The buck could no longer feel; its fighting was a mechanical protest of the nerves. But it was not that which made him put down the gun. It was a swelling feeling of rage and misery and protest that expressed itself in the thought: if I had not come it would have died like this, so why should I interfere? All over the bush things like this happen; they happen all the time; this is how life goes on, by living things dying in anguish. I can't stop it. I can't stop it. There is nothing I can do.

He was glad that the buck was unconscious and had gone past suffering so that he did not have to make a decision to kill it. At his feet, now, were ants trickling back with pink fragments in their mouths, and there was a fresh acid smell in his nose. He sternly controlled the uselessly convulsing muscles of his empty stomach, and reminded himself: the ants must eat too!

The shape had grown small. Now it looked like nothing recognisable. He did not know how long it was before he saw the blackness thin, and bits of white showed through, shining in the sun – yes, there was the sun just up, glowing over the rocks. Why, the whole thing could not have taken longer than a few minutes.

He strode forward, crushing ants with each step, and brushing them off his clothes, till he stood above the skeleton. It was clean-picked. It might have been lying there years, except that on the white bone there were pink fragments of flesh. About the bones ants were ebbing away, their pincers full of meat.

The boy looked at them, big black ugly insects. A few were standing and gazing up at him with small glittering eyes.

'Go away!' he said to the ants very coldly. 'I am not for you – not just yet, at any rate. Go away.' And he fancied that the ants turned and went away.

He bent over the bones and touched the sockets in the skull: that was where the eyes were, he thought incredulously, remembering the liquid dark eyes of a buck.

That morning, perhaps an hour ago, this small creature had been stepping proud and free through the bush, feeling the chill on its skin even as he himself had done, exhilarated by it. Proudly stepping the earth, frisking a pretty white tail, it had sniffed the cold morning air. Walking like kings and conquerors it had moved freely 40 through this bush, where each blade of grass grew for it alone, and where the river ran pure sparkling water for it to drink.

And then – what had happened? Such a sure swiftfooted thing could surely not be trapped by a swarm of ants?

(From *A Sunrise on the Veld* by Doris Lessing)

Multiple choice

Read the passage carefully, then answer the following questions.
Choose the response which best reflects the meaning of the text.

1 When the boy first saw the buck it was
a) already dead.
b) still on its feet.
c) lying on the ground dying.
d) struggling in a muddy stream.

2 He did not shoot the buck because
a) he did not want to hurt it.
b) the buck was unconscious.
c) he did not want to interfere with the laws of the bush.
d) he did not want to have its death on his conscience.

3 When the boy saw the ants carrying away the 'pink fragments' (line 20)
a) he began to feel hungry.
b) he felt guilty for not having shot the buck.
c) he was glad that the ants would have something to eat.
d) he was almost overcome with disgust.

4 By the time the ants had picked the skeleton clean it was
a) late afternoon.
b) close to midday.
c) just after dawn.
d) already dark.

5 The main idea in the last 10 lines of the passage is that
a) the boy cannot understand how the buck could have suddenly lost its life.
b) he suddenly remembers a buck he had once shot in the early morning.
c) he does not believe that ants are capable of killing a buck.
d) he identifies himself with the buck as a free creature of the bush.

True or false?

Without looking back at the text, decide whether the following statements are true or false.

1 As soon as the boy came near the buck the ants attacked him.

Reading comprehension: Unit 18

2 The buck was trapped in mud.
3 The boy could see the ants but not hear them.
4 The boy did not shoot the buck.
5 There was nothing extraordinary about the buck's death.
6 The ants left nothing of the animal except the bones.
7 The buck was devoured in a few minutes.
8 The boy was frightened by the ants.
9 It was a hot morning.
10 The boy did not believe that the ants alone could have killed the buck.

Vocabulary in context

Choose the definition which best fits these words or phrases as they are used in the text.

1 *convulsively* (line 8)
a) in spasms
b) violently
c) painfully
d) without strength

2 *twitches* (line 9)
a) cries of pain
b) uncontrolled movements
c) breathless gasps
d) uncovered patches

3 *fragments* (lines 20, 29)
a) patches of blood
b) little bits of meat
c) pieces of grass
d) drops of water

4 *anguish* (line 17)
a) helplessness
b) secret
c) great pain
d) sudden attacks

5 *ebbing away* (line 30)
a) hurrying off
b) turning back
c) retreating
d) struggling

6 '*I am not for you . . .*' (line 33)
a) I do not like you
b) I am not ready to die
c) I am not interested in you
d) I am not frightened of you

Reading comprehension: Unit 18

7 *incredulously* (line 36)
a) disbelievingly
b) unhappily
c) seriously
d) indecisively

8 *exhilarated* (line 39)
a) chilled
b) refreshed
c) invigorated
d) astonished

Unit 19

The secrets of sleep

The secrets of sleep were a mystery for centuries simply because there was neither the means to explore them, nor the need. Only when candles gave way to gaslight, and gas to electricity, when man became able to convert night into day, and double his output by working shifts round the clock, did people seriously start wondering if sleep could possibly be a waste of time. Our ability to switch night into day is very recent, and it is questionable if we will ever either want, or be able, to give up our habit of enjoying a good night's sleep. However, a remarkable research project in London has already discovered a few people who actually enjoy insomnia. Even chronic insomniacs often get hours more sleep than they think. But, by placing electric contacts beside the eyes and on the head, it is possible to check their complaint by studying the tiny currents we generate which reveal the different brainwaves of sleep and wakefulness. This has shown that for some people seven or eight hours of sleep a night are quite unnecessary.

A lot of recent work has shown that too much sleep is bad for you, so that if you are fortunate enough to be born with a body which needs only a small amount of sleep, you may well be healthier and happier than someone who sleeps longer.

Every attempt to unravel the secrets of sleep, and be precise about its function, raises many problems. The sleeper himself cannot tell what is going on and, even when he wakes, has only a very hazy idea of how good or bad a night he has had. The research is expensive and often unpopular, as it inevitably involves working at night. Only in the last few years have experts come up with theories about the function of sleep and the laws which may govern it.

The real advance in sleep research came in 1937 with the use of the electroencephalogram. This machine showed small – 50 microvolt – changes in the brain, so, for the first time, we could observe sleep from moment to moment. Before that time one could put the person to bed, watch him mumble, toss, turn, bring back a few rough memories of dreams, and that was about all. In 1937 it was possible to read out these changes, second by second. Then in 1959 two other things happened. Kleitman and Aserinsky, as they were looking at eye movements, trying to understand the brainwaves, noticed that after about ninety minutes there would be a burst of the EEG, as if the person was awake, and the eyes would move rapidly. It was not hard to guess that maybe that was a dream. And indeed it was. Waking people up during that period, they found they were dreaming; waking them up at other periods, they found no dreams.

The electroencephalograph shows that when we fall asleep we pass through a cycle of sleep stages. At the onset of sleep, the cycle lasts about ninety minutes during which you pass through stages one, two and three to stage four. This is the deepest form of sleep, and from it you retreat to stage two, and from there into REM, or rapid eye

Reading comprehension: Unit 19

movement sleep. Here, for ten minutes on the first cycle and then gradually longer, it is thought that we do most of our dreaming. 40

Studies of people who volunteered to be locked up for weeks in an observation chamber with no idea of whether it is night or day, give remarkable results. We are not, in fact, twenty-four-hour creatures. Put people in such circumstances and, even though the patterns of sleep continue, the day is extended to about twenty-five and a half hours. Without any clues to time, these people go to sleep the first night about 45 an hour later than usual, the next night an hour later, *and* the next night. So that, after about ten days, the person is going to sleep at three o'clock in the afternoon, thinking that he is still going to sleep at midnight.

Today, jet-lag is a familiar hazard for the seasoned traveller. Travel across time zones plays havoc with the biological clock rhythms of the human body. For the active 50 pilot, who is rarely in one place long enough to know if it is time for breakfast or dinner, the impact of jet-lag on his sleep is critical. Several air disasters have been partly caused by overtired pilots ignoring the natural laws of sleep. Much research is directed to finding out what these laws are and to what extent pilots and astronauts dare disobey them. But they are laws which affect all of us, not just pilots. 55
(From an article in *The Listener*)

Multiple choice

Read the passage carefully, then answer the following questions.
Choose the response which best reflects the meaning of the text.

1 Only after the invention of electricity did people start
a) to really enjoy insomnia.
b) asking themselves if sleep was a waste of time.
c) to need to do research into sleep.
d) giving up the habit of sleeping so much.

2 It seems that most people
a) need a lot of sleep.
b) sleep too much.
c) need less sleep than we thought.
d) need more sleep than we thought.

3 The electroencephalogram records
a) eye movements.
b) the frequency of dreams.
c) the time it takes to have a dream.
d) small currents in the brain.

4 Dreams seem to be associated with
a) deep sleep.
b) rapid eye movements.
c) jet-lag.
d) overtiredness.

5 The people in the observation chamber
a) went to sleep an hour earlier than usual each night.
b) started to go to bed in the afternoon.

Reading comprehension: Unit 19

c) slept for a much longer period than usual.
d) went to sleep about an hour later than usual.

6 *Jet-lag* (line 49) means
a) being unable to sleep properly on aeroplanes.
b) the clock says it is one time and the body says it is another.
c) it is a different time in different parts of the world.
d) prolonging the day from twenty-four hours to twenty-five and a half hours.

True or false?

Without looking back at the text, decide whether the following statements are true or false.

1 We shall probably want, and be able, to give up sleeping in the future.
2 People who suffer from insomnia often get much more sleep than they imagine.
3 If you only sleep a little you are certainly healthier than someone who sleeps a lot.
4 Research into sleep is now quite easy.
5 When people dream, their eyes move.
6 The cycle of sleep-stages lasts ten minutes.
7 When people are kept in a room and do not know what time it is, they tend to continue to go to sleep at the same time.
8 Air disasters are generally caused by jet-lag.
9 Jet-lag destroys the appetite.
10 The laws of sleep only affect pilots.

Vocabulary in context

Choose the definition which best fits these words or phrases as they are used in the text.

1 *gave way to* (line 2)
a) were rejected in favour of
b) gradually replaced
c) were replaced by
d) came back into use after

2 Which of the following is *not* a suitable alternative for *convert*? (line 3)
a) change
b) turn
c) alter
d) transform

3 *chronic insomniacs* (line 8)
a) people who enjoy not sleeping
b) people who regularly do not sleep
c) people who sleep more than most insomniacs
d) people who occasionally cannot sleep

4 *unravel* (line 17)
a) disentangle
b) disrupt

c) disturb
d) discredit

5 *have . . . come up with* (line 21)
a) rejected
b) questioned
c) produced
d) confirmed

6 *clues* (line 45)
a) clockwork
b) certainty
c) assistance
d) information

7 *seasoned traveller* (line 49)
a) someone who travels at certain times of the year only
b) someone who is accustomed to travelling
c) someone who does not like travelling
d) someone who suffers from travelling

8 *impact* (line 52)
a) result
b) loss
c) effect
d) cause

Summary

Go through the text paragraph by paragraph, picking out the main points. Then write a summary. Try to limit yourself to *two* sentences for each paragraph.

Unit 20

The dangers of space

Space is a dangerous place, not only because of meteors but also because of rays from the sun and other stars. The atmosphere again acts as our protective blanket on earth. Light gets through, and this is essential for plants to make the food which we eat. Heat, too, makes our environments tolerable and some ultraviolet rays penetrate the atmosphere. Cosmic rays of various kinds come through the air from outer space, but enormous quantities of radiation from the sun are screened off. As soon as men leave the atmosphere they are exposed to this radiation but their spacesuits or the walls of their spacecraft, if they are inside, do prevent a lot of radiation damage.

Radiation is the greatest known danger to explorers in space. Doses of radiation are measured in units called 'rems'. We all receive radiation here on Earth from the sun, from cosmic rays and from radioactive minerals. The 'normal' dose of radiation that we receive each year is about 100 millirems (0.1 rem); it varies according to where you live, and this is a very rough estimate. Scientists have reason to think that a man can put up with far more radiation than this without being damaged; the figure of 60 rems has been agreed. The trouble is that it is extremely difficult to be sure about radiation damage – a person may feel perfectly well, but the cells of his or her sex organs may be damaged, and this will not be discovered until the birth of (deformed) children or even grandchildren.

Early space probes showed that radiation varies in different parts of space around the Earth. It also varies in time because, when great spurts of gas shoot out of the sun (solar flares), they are accompanied by a lot of extra radiation. Some estimates of the amount of radiation in space, based on various measurements and calculations, are as low as 10 rems per year, others are as high as 5 rems per hour! Missions to the moon (the Apollo flights) have had to cross the Van Allen belts of high radiation and, during the outward and return journeys, the Apollo 8 crew accumulated a total dose of about 200 millirems per man. It was hoped that there would not be any large solar flares during the times of the Apollo moon walks because the walls of the LEMs (lunar excursion modules) were not thick enough to protect the men inside, though the command modules did give reasonable protection. So far, no dangerous doses of radiation have been reported, but the Gemini orbits and the Apollo missions have been quite short. We simply do not know yet how men are going to get on when they spend weeks and months outside the protection of the atmosphere, working in a space laboratory or in a base on the moon. Drugs might help to decrease the damage done by radiation, but no really effective ones have been found so far. At present, radiation seems to be the greatest physical hazard to space travellers, but it is impossible to say just how serious the hazard will turn out to be in the future.
(From *Space Biology* by C. F. Stoneman)

Reading comprehension: Unit 20

Multiple choice

Read the passage carefully, then answer the following questions. Choose the response which best reflects the meaning of the text.

1 The worst hazard for spacemen is
a) meteors.
b) heat.
c) radiation.
d) gas.

2 Scientists have fixed a safety level of
a) 10 rems per year.
b) 60 rems per year.
c) 100 millirems per year.
d) 5 rems per hour.

3 The spacemen were worried about solar flares when they were
a) crossing the Van Allen belts.
b) setting up a moon base.
c) exploring the surface of the moon.
d) waiting in the command module.

4 When men spend long periods in space how will they protect themselves?
a) By taking special drugs.
b) By wearing special suits.
c) By using a protective blanket.
d) No solution has been found yet.

5 Which of the following is true?
a) The grandchildren of astronauts are deformed.
b) The children of astronauts have damaged sex organs.
c) Radiation damage may show only in later generations.
d) Radiation does not seem to be very harmful.

True or false?

Without looking back at the text, decide whether the following statements are true or false.

1 The atmosphere screens off the Earth from excessive radiation.
2 Spacesuits help to prevent radiation damage.
3 Meteors are the main danger in space.
4 Everyone on Earth is exposed to exactly the same amount of radiation.
5 It is easy to tell if a person has been damaged by radiation
6 Solar flares are not dangerous.
7 Command modules are safer than lunar excursion modules.
8 Several astronauts have had serious radiation illness.
9 Drugs will decrease radiation damage.
10 Scientists have worked out ways of preventing radiation damage.

Reading comprehension: Unit 20

Vocabulary in context

Choose the definition which best fits these words or phrases as they are used in the text.

1 *cosmic rays* (lines 5, 11)
a) rays from outer space
b) sunbeams
c) ultraviolet rays
d) rays from spacecraft

2 *screened off* (line 6)
a) taken away
b) soaked up
c) kept away
d) passed through

3 *put up with* (line 14)
a) raise
b) tolerate
c) expect
d) produce

4 *Scientists have reason to think . . .* (line 13)
a) Scientists are right to think . . .
b) Scientists have evidence to suggest . . .
c) Scientists need to think . . .
d) Scientists are certain . . .

5 *get on* (line 31)
a) mount
b) walk
c) survive
d) advance

6 *turn out to be* (line 36)
a) change
b) harm
c) remain
d) prove

Summary

Write a summary of the passage in *seven* sentences. Remember that only important facts should be included. Here are some possible guidelines:
– The atmosphere . . . so that . . . as in space, where men . . .
– The greatest . . . which . . .
– Scientists can only . . . because . . .
– Radiation varies in . . . and in . . . because . . .
– Astronauts have been exposed . . . and it was hoped . . .
– So far . . . and no . . . but when . . .
– At present . . .

Listening comprehension

Unit 1

Three sacks of carrots

A passage will either be read to you twice by your teacher or played on a recording. Listen carefully both times and then answer the following questions. Choose the response which best reflects the meaning of the text.

1 Jim, the Englishman
a) was studying the life of Pygmies in New Guinea.
b) was working for a European firm in central New Guinea.
c) was living alone in the mountains of New Guinea.
d) was running a store in the mountains of New Guinea.

2 Jim was not surprised when the party arrived because
a) one of the porters had gone on ahead to tell him they were coming.
b) he received regular visits from people coming up from the coast.
c) he heard the porters singing on their way down the mountain.
d) he had been informed by radio that someone was coming.

3 When Jim brought out the claret his guests
a) were amazed because they did not expect to find wine in central New Guinea.
b) were disappointed because they would have preferred whisky.
c) were suspicious because they did not believe it was real wine.
d) were delighted because they were tired of drinking whisky.

4 Sixty bottles of claret were dropped to Jim because
a) the doctor had told him it would improve his eyesight.
b) the man at the store had run out of carrots.
c) Jim preferred wine to carrots.
d) the man at the store thought Jim had made a mistake.

True or false?

Listen to the passage again, then decide whether the following statements are true or false.

1 Jim had been working for a European company for six years in New Guinea.
2 Jim got on well with the local people.
3 Jim's English had got worse in New Guinea.
4 He was pleased to see his visitors.
5 The hut in which Jim lived was spotlessly clean.
6 The visitors would not have been surprised if Jim had offered them whisky.

Listening comprehension: Unit 2

7 Jim saw the doctor every month.
8 The doctor thought that Jim's eyesight was getting weak.
9 Jim was too lazy to grow carrots.
10 The bottles of claret were dropped to Jim from an aeroplane.
11 The visitors drank only very little of the wine.
12 Jim never drank wine.

Vocabulary in context

How well did you understand the following phrases when you heard them? Choose the most accurate definition.

1 *a very good working relationship with the local people*
a) he worked well with the local people
b) he made the local people work well
c) he was on good terms with the local people
d) he was admired by the local people for his work

2 *remotest New Guinea*
a) the most mountainous part of New Guinea
b) the least civilized part of New Guinea
c) the least dangerous part of New Guinea
d) the most distant part of New Guinea

3 *'What you want, Jim . . .'*
a) what you need
b) what you like
c) what you asked for
d) what you must avoid

4 *We tucked into his claret*
a) we tasted his wine out of politeness
b) we drank as much as we could of his wine
c) we put some bottles into our bags
d) we turned down his offer of a drink

5 *that particular problem*
a) the problem of how to find some carrots
b) the problem of how to finish the wine
c) the problem of working out why wine had been sent instead of carrots
d) the problem of how to improve his eyesight

Unit 2

Darwin ruined by Cyclone Tracy

Multiple choice

A passage will either be read to you twice by your teacher or played on a recording. Listen carefully both times and then answer the following questions. Choose the response which best reflects the meaning of the text.

Listening comprehension: Unit 2

1 The inhabitants of Darwin ignored the cyclone warning because
a) Darwin does not lie in the Australian cyclone belt.
b) cyclones rarely hit their town.
c) it was Christmas Eve and few people were at home.
d) the houses were all strongly built.

2 Two weeks before Christmas Day
a) Darwin was hit by a cyclone.
b) the first warning of the Cyclone Tracy was given.
c) Townsville was devastated.
d) a cyclone passed close to Darwin.

3 Most people who were killed in the cyclone died because
a) they were travelling in their cars.
b) their houses were not strongly built.
c) Darwin lies in the most dangerous cyclone belt.
d) the storm came unexpectedly.

4 After Townsville was devastated by a cyclone the Darwin authorities
a) took measures to improve the standard of construction.
b) built special tropical huts.
c) took no notice of the new regulations.
d) followed the example of the other Australian states.

True or false?

Listen to the passage again, then decide whether the following statements are true or false.

1 Darwin lies on the south coast of Australia.
2 The people of Darwin knew nothing of the approach of Cyclone Tracy.
3 In December 1971 Darwin was seriously damaged by a cyclone.
4 Australian coastal towns are not often hit by cyclones.
5 There was no time to warn the people of Darwin of the approach of the cyclone.
6 After the cyclone in 1971 building standards were changed in most states.
7 Darwin has a tropical climate.

Vocabulary in context

How well did you understand the following words or phrases when you heard them? Choose the most accurate definition.

1 *evacuating*
a) receiving
b) removing
c) vaccinating
d) rescuing

2 *devastated*
a) damaged
b) destroyed
c) affected
d) hit

Listening comprehension: Unit 3

3 *sparking off*
a) provoking
b) requiring
c) silencing
d) supporting

4 *headed off*
a) broke up
b) came to an end
c) went on
d) turned back

5 *withstand*
a) overcome
b) resist
c) test
d) deflect

6 *consequently*
a) nevertheless
b) besides
c) therefore
d) since

Unit 3

Speeding

Multiple choice

A passage will either be read to you twice by your teacher or played on a recording. Listen carefully both times and then answer the following questions. Choose the response which best reflects the meaning of the text.

1 Under the old Locomotives Act
a) you could not drive in town unless a man with a red flag was walking in front of your car.
b) you did not need to have a man with a red flag provided you drove under 2 m.p.h.
c) if you wanted to drive faster than 2 m.p.h. you had to have a man with a red flag in front of your car.
d) you did not need a man with a red flag provided you drove slower than 4 m.p.h.

2 Between 1930 and 1935
a) many new traffic regulations were introduced.
b) no great changes were made.
c) nobody observed the speed limits.
d) no speed limits existed.

3 Exceeding the limit on a restricted road means
a) driving too fast in the country.
b) driving too fast in a built-up area.

Listening comprehension: Unit 3

c) driving too fast for the class your vehicle belongs to.
d) driving too fast on a badly lit road.

4 The Transport Ministry believes that
a) most bad accidents are caused by speeding.
b) speed limits have caused an increase in bad accidents.
c) speed limits should be abolished.
d) there are fewer bad accidents when there is a speed limit.

5 In America it is thought that
a) the more cars there are the more accidents there will be.
b) the fewer cars there are the more accidents there will be.
c) the more cars there are the fewer accidents there will be.
d) the fewer cars there are the fewer accidents there will be.

True or false?

Listen to the passage again, then decide whether the following statements are true or false.

1 Before 1903 there was no speed limit.
2 Speed limits were abolished around 1930 because they were no longer needed.
3 Driving tests were started in 1935.
4 A restricted road is one on which the distance between the street lamps is not greater than 200 yards.
5 When the 30 m.p.h. speed limit was introduced in 1935 fatal accidents increased by 15 per cent.
6 In America it has been proved that speed limits reduce the number of fatal accidents.
7 In parts of America you do not have to observe the speed limits.

Vocabulary in context

How well did you understand the following words or phrases when you heard them? Choose the most accurate definition.

1 *taken to court*
a) presented to the Queen
b) brought before a judge
c) escorted into the city
d) imprisoned in the Tower

2 *summoned*
a) called for trial
b) decorated for his services
c) fined for speeding
d) publicised in the press

3 *ignored*
a) misunderstood
b) enforced
c) broken
d) accepted

Listening comprehension: Unit 4

4 *trifles*
a) personal quarrels
b) petty details
c) statistical research
d) false evidence

5 *controversy*
a) weakness
b) difficulty
c) dispute
d) interest

6 *casualties*
a) injuries
b) arrests
c) crashes
d) breakdowns

Unit 4

The reality of being a detective

Multiple choice

A passage will either be read to you twice by your teacher or played on a recording. Listen carefully both times and then answer the following questions. Choose the response which best reflects the meaning of the text.

1 One of the great differences between television cops and real-life detectives is that
a) real-life detectives are happily married.
b) television detectives are never married.
c) real-life detectives are often in bad condition.
d) television detectives are not as tough as they seem.

2 Detectives in specialist units
a) are not interested in anything outside their speciality.
b) are not allowed to work on general crime cases.
c) prefer to concentrate on one type of crime.
d) find that they are forgotten when it comes to promotion.

3 By comparison with their British counterparts, American detectives
a) are more active.
b) have less formal training.
c) make more arrests on the street.
d) are slower to learn their trade.

4 After sixteen weeks' basic training the British detective
a) has to join the CID.
b) has to attend criminal trials in court for two years.

Listening comprehension: Unit 4

c) has to spend two years doing routine police work.
d) has to pass a special examination.

5 American detectives do not have to rely entirely on their salaries because
a) they are better paid than British detectives.
b) they get paid extra for all their convictions.
c) they accept money from criminals.
d) they have private incomes.

True or false?

Listen to the passage again, then decide whether the following statements are true or false.

1 The marriages of British detectives are often unsuccessful.
2 Detectives have great difficulty in falling asleep.
3 It is difficult to compare the work of detectives in different countries.
4 After training, British detectives are automatically accepted into the CID.
5 At the detective training school 80 per cent of the candidates pass the examinations.
6 Students are given lectures in murder and explosives because these are considered the most important parts of their training.
7 American detectives gain most of their practical experience in the streets.
8 It is surprising that American detectives earn more than their British counterparts.
9 Corruption is not unknown among American policemen.

Vocabulary in context

How well did you understand the following words or phrases when you heard them? Choose the most accurate definition.

1 *shaky affairs*
a) unstable
b) dangerous
c) suspicious
d) lighthearted

2 *assigned*
a) attracted
b) appointed
c) suited
d) trained

3 *the rest of the world passes him by*
a) everybody ignores him
b) he loses interest in the world
c) he ignores all other types of crime
d) everybody comes to consult him about his speciality

4 *on the beat*
a) out of work
b) chasing criminals

Listening comprehension: Unit 5

    c) patrolling the streets
    d) undergoing special training

5 *as a diversion*
    a) for the sake of amusement
    b) in order to distract their attention
    c) as a special privilege
    d) by way of an examination

6 *hard grind*
    a) highly technical studying
    b) tedious repetition
    c) intensive work
    d) pure criminal law

7 *in earnest*
    a) seriously
    b) in secret
    c) properly
    d) in plain clothes

8 *fired*
    a) accused of corruption
    b) dismissed from their jobs
    c) discovered accepting money
    d) wrongly charged

9 *underworld*
    a) mining companies
    b) unknown sources
    c) gangsters and criminals
    d) special allowances

Unit 5

The curse of the islands

True or false?

After listening carefully to the text, decide whether the following statements are true or false.
  1 The Shetland Islands suffered economically before the discovery of oil.
  2 Most of the fish caught is processed in the Shetland Islands.
  3 The Shetlanders sell more haddock to Western Europe than to anywhere else.
  4 There are already large numbers of oilmen in the Shetlands.
  5 There is plenty of room for ships to unload in the Shetlands.
  6 The fishing and knitwear industries have been wrecked by the oil boom.
  7 Beaches in the Shetlands have been polluted by oil spillage.
  8 The fishing and knitwear industries matter less than the oil industry.

Listening comprehension: Unit 6

9 Courage and imagination are qualities typical of the Shetlanders.
10 The Shetlanders are afraid that people will leave the local industries.
11 Most Shetland fishermen own their own boats.

Multiple choice

Now listen to the passage once again.
In the following questions, choose the response which best reflects the meaning of the text.

1 Fish processing factories are profitable because
a) the fish does not go to Aberdeen.
b) the oil boom has expanded the markets.
c) fish prices have risen.
d) there has been an expansion of demand abroad.

2 The favourite national snack in the USA is
a) hamburgers.
b) haddock.
c) fish and chips.
d) cod.

3 How many oilmen are there on Shetland?
a) a lot
b) a few
c) one
d) none

4 If men from Shetland go to work in the oil industry, what will happen?
a) The fishing boats will not be able to unload quickly enough.
b) Local industries will be ruined.
c) The beaches will be polluted.
d) The local industries will enjoy a boom.

5 The beaches on Shetland
a) will probably be polluted.
b) have been polluted.
c) will not be polluted.
d) are being polluted.

Unit 6

Colour and feelings

Multiple choice

A passage will either be read to you twice by your teacher or played on a recording.
Listen carefully both times and then answer the following questions.
Choose the response which best reflects the meaning of the text.

Listening comprehension: Unit 6

1 Manufacturers found out that colour affects sales
a) by experience over a long period of time.
b) by experimenting with different colours.
c) by trying out colours on blind people.
d) by developing the discipline of colour psychology.

2 Our preferences for certain colours are
a) associated with the time of day.
b) partly due to psychological factors.
c) dependent on our character.
d) linked with our primitive ancestors.

3 If people are exposed to bright red, which of the following things does *not* happen?
a) They breathe faster.
b) Their blood pressure rises.
c) They feel afraid.
d) Their hearts beat faster.

4 The most effective colour for warning people is
a) red.
b) green.
c) blue.
d) yellow.

True or false?

Listen to the passage again, then decide whether the following statements are true or false.

1 Colour probably has an effect on us which we are not conscious of.
2 Manufacturers know that certain colours are bad for sales.
3 Sugar sells very well in blue wrappings.
4 Food should never be packaged in brown.
5 The psychology of colour is of no practical use.
6 Our feelings about certain colours are purely psychological.
7 Yellow is the complementary colour to red.
8 People exposed to pure blue start to breathe more slowly.
9 Yellow fire engines have caused many bad accidents.

Vocabulary in context

1 There is a word in the passage which means 'tastes bad'. Which is it?
a) unperishable
b) unpalatal
c) unpalatable
d) unpalpable

2 *Passivity*. Which word in the passage means the opposite of this word?
a) energy
b) self-preservation
c) defence
d) alarm

Listening comprehension: Unit 7

3 *Trial and error* means
a) on and off methods
b) give and take methods
c) down and out methods
d) hit and miss methods

4 Here is a shape:

Which of these shapes is *complementary* to it?

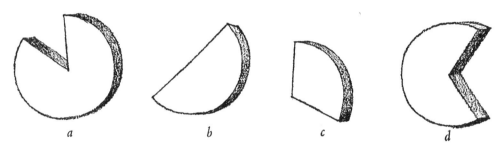

Unit 7

Pizarro and the Inca gold

Multiple choice

A passage will either be read to you twice by your teacher or played on a recording. Listen carefully both times and then answer the following questions. Choose the response which best reflects the meaning of the text.

1 When the news of the Inca gold first reached Spain
a) it aroused great excitement.
b) it was received with some scepticism.
c) it gave rise to fierce quarrels among the rulers.
d) it was completely ignored.

2 On his first voyage south from Panama, Pizarro
a) was captured by natives.
b) discovered an empire rich in gold.
c) was forced to turn back by storms.
d) sailed into unknown regions.

Listening comprehension: Unit 7

3 King Charles V of Spain
a) was reluctant to let Pizarro make a third voyage.
b) gave Pizarro full financial support for his third voyage.
c) refused to allow Pizarro to make his third voyage.
d) did not believe Pizarro's report.

4 Pizarro was encouraged by the news of the civil war, because
a) he wanted to kill the Sapa Inca.
b) his army was too weak to march properly.
c) he hoped to profit from the confusion.
d) the Incas no longer had a leader.

5 Pizarro finally
a) went back to Spain and died a rich man.
b) died fighting in Peru.
c) returned to Spain and was ruined financially.
d) suffered serious injuries from which he died.

True or false?

Listen to the passage again, then decide whether the following statements are true or false.

1 The exact date of Pizarro's birth is not known.
2 Pizarro was a member of the exploration party which discovered the Pacific.
3 Pizarro did not believe the rumour of the Inca gold.
4 King Charles V would not help Pizarro to pay for his third voyage.
5 When Pizarro landed at Tumbez he learnt that he would have to march a thousand miles to reach the Sapa Inca.
6 The Spaniards were merciless in their treatment of the Incas.
7 Pizarro had the full support of his men.
8 Spain would not have been ruined financially if it had been able to get more gold.

Vocabulary in context

How well did you understand the following words or phrases when you heard them? Choose the most accurate definition.

1 *illegitimate*
a) a juvenile delinquent
b) born of unmarried parents
c) poorly educated
d) a political refugee

2 *discounted*
a) ignored
b) dismissed
c) recounted
d) accepted

Listening comprehension: Unit 8

3 *beat his way*
a) sailed very fast
b) discovered a new route
c) was driven off course
d) progressed with difficulty

4 *crude*
a) rough
b) rare
c) worthless
d) strange

5 *grasped*
a) acknowledged
b) realised
c) accepted
d) believed

6 *with the death of the Inca chief*
a) while the Inca chief was dying
b) after the Inca chief had died
c) having killed the Inca chief
d) owing to the death of the Inca chief

7 *inevitably*
a) finally
b) unavoidably
c) eventually
d) unfortunately

8 *surfeit*
a) inflow
b) profit
c) excess
d) discovery

Unit 8

A formidable sound

Multiple choice

A passage will either be read to you twice by your teacher or played on a recording. Listen carefully both times and then answer the following questions.
Choose the response which best reflects the meaning of the text.

1 Professor Gavraud felt ill because
a) there were chemicals in his room.
b) his office was too high up.

c) he was affected by vibrations.
d) he was a very sensitive man.

2 He constructed a very large copy of a police whistle because he wanted to
a) produce low-frequency sounds.
b) improve its design.
c) compare it with an organ.
d) see the effect it had on people.

3 The first experiment with the machine
a) caused a major earthquake.
b) broke all the windows in nearby buildings.
c) made a noise like an organ.
d) killed the man who switched it on.

4 In his second experiment Professor Gavraud took some precautions. Which of the following precautions was *not* taken?
a) The observers were protected by a concrete shelter.
b) The experiment was done outside.
c) The compressed air was turned on slowly.
d) A smaller machine was used.

5 What other interesting discovery did he make?
a) That windows can be broken very easily.
b) That two machines aimed at one place are very powerful.
c) That the machines are not very expensive to produce.
d) That it is possible to control the power of the infrasound.

True or false?

Listen to the passage again, then decide whether the following statements are true or false.

1 Professor Gavraud left his job because he felt sick.
2 The cause of his sickness was not in the room.
3 He had a bicycle in his office.
4 The air-conditioning plant had nothing to do with his sickness.
5 He constructed a very big organ.
6 The result of the first trial was very worrying.
7 He did his second test indoors.
8 The air was turned on quickly.
9 He was trying to break windows with his machine.
10 Later on he designed even bigger generators.
11 Low-frequency waves can be directed at a particular point a long way away.
12 Two generators which are focused are as powerful as a small earthquake.
13 These machines cost a lot of money to build.

Vocabulary in context

How well did you understand the following words or phrases when you heard them? Choose the most accurate definition.

Listening comprehension: Unit 8

1 *infrasound*
a) high-frequency sound
b) low-frequency sound
c) medium-frequency sound

2 *to track down*
a) to smell
b) to detect
c) to examine
d) to remove

3 *devices*
a) instruments
b) inventions
c) substances
d) tools

4 *to give up*
a) to go on
b) to stop
c) to collapse
d) to find out

5 *turned out to be*
a) was shown to be
b) was intended to be
c) was thought to be
d) was known to be

6 *casting around*
a) looking for
b) hoping for
c) asking for
d) sending for

7 *went ahead*
a) delayed
b) proceeded
c) hurried
d) changed

8 *The infrasound generator* means the machine which generates infrasound. Which of the following words is commonly associated with 'generator'?
a) gas
b) coal
c) water
d) electricity

Listening comprehension: Unit 9

9 In which of these examples are machines A and B resonating 'in sympathy' with each other?

Machine A	Machine B
a) 7 cycles per second	7 cycles per second
b) 7 cycles per second	14 cycles per second
c) 14 cycles per second	20 cycles per second

Unit 9

The stamping of the thorns

Multiple choice

A passage will either be read to you twice by your teacher or played on a recording. Listen carefully both times and then answer the following questions. Choose the response which best reflects the meaning of the text.

1 The saying 'It is the master's eye which makes the cow grow fat', means
a) one should always be on one's guard.
b) one should always mind one's own business.
c) one should not leave one's own work to others.
d) he suffered from a mental illness.

2 Shaka's new *assegai* was
a) easier to throw than the old one.
b) not designed for throwing.
c) was not as strong as the old one.
d) designed after a spear once used by the Zulus.

3 Shaka's soldiers
a) welcomed the idea of going barefoot.
b) refused absolutely to go barefoot.
c) were unwilling to go barefoot.
d) did not believe that Shaka seriously wanted them to go barefoot.

4 Shaka wanted his men to harden their feet because
a) he knew it would make them quicker in battle.
b) he wanted to prove how tough he was.
c) he wanted an excuse to kill off some of his men.
d) he was a kind and helpful leader.

5 During the stamping
a) half of Shaka's regiment was killed by the slayers.
b) half of the men in the front rank were killed by the slayers.
c) only six men were killed by the slayers.
d) six men from each rank were killed by the slayers.

True or false?

Listen to the passage again, then decide whether the following statements are true or false.

Listening comprehension: Unit 10

1 Shaka was an extremely careful man.
2 When Shaka first called his regiments together he had an army of no more than 5000 men.
3 Shaka's new *assegai* was popular with the younger soldiers.
4 Shaka's soldiers objected to his order to throw away their sandals.
5 Shaka himself did everything he asked his men to do.
6 'Devil thorns' are the same shape as the thorns of a rose.
7 Shaka did not feel the thorns because he was wearing sandals.
8 Shaka killed only those men who did not stamp hard enough.
9 Shaka did not let his men go until the thorns could no longer be seen.

Vocabulary in context

How well did you understand the following words or phrases when you heard them? Choose the most accurate definition.

1 *invariably*
a) easily
b) occasionally
c) carefully
d) regularly

2 *took up*
a) adopted
b) held
c) threw
d) discussed

3 *it has come to my ears*
a) I am tired of hearing
b) I cannot believe
c) it has been brought to my notice
d) I have the impression

4 *gritted their teeth*
a) showed their anger
b) called up their courage
c) smiled unhappily
d) bit their tongues

Unit 10

Recycling waste

Multiple choice

A passage will either be read to you twice by your teacher or played on a recording. Listen carefully both times and then answer the following questions.
Choose the response which best reflects the meaning of the text.

1 Projects for recycling waste in Britain
a) will not be started for at least fifteen years.
b) are being developed all over Britain.

Listening comprehension: Unit 10

c) have not yet been fully tested.
d) have been abandoned because they are too expensive.

2 The purpose of the latest recycling project is
a) to prevent people from putting rubbish into holes.
b) to find a way of destroying all kinds of waste.
c) to extract useful raw materials from the waste.
d) to find out how much raw material is being wasted.

3 The new type of recycling plant will
a) recycle only paper and rubber.
b) not recycle metals, paper or rubber.
c) recycle paper, rubber and metals.
d) not recycle steel, lead or copper.

4 The first recycling plants
a) have already been built in large industrial areas.
b) will not be built for at least fifteen years.
c) will probably be built in the next fifteen years.
d) will be too expensive to build near big cities.

True or false?

Listen to the passage again, then decide whether the following statements are true or false.

1 Britain is not the only nation that is planning to recycle waste.
2 Most rubbish is dangerous and cannot be re-used.
3 Warren Spring is in the North of England.
4 The new recycling plants will be built far away from cities.
5 The new recycling plants will be able to process most kinds of waste.
6 Magnets will be used to separate the iron from the steel.
7 Rubber and plastic are the last materials to be sorted out.
8 Recycling plants will be necessary because it is now too expensive to transport rubbish.

Vocabulary in context

How well did you understand the following words or phrases when you heard them? Choose the most accurate definition.

1 *well on with*
a) nearing completion
b) getting ready to start
c) making improvements on
d) finished with

2 *taking shape*
a) attracting interest
b) making progress
c) proving difficult
d) being examined

Listening comprehension: Unit 11

3 *raw* (materials)
a) unprocessed
b) waste
c) rare
d) recycled

4 *just outside the city*
a) outside the city and nowhere else
b) close to the city boundary
c) round the edge of the city
d) a long way from the city

5 *dumped*
a) destroyed
b) deposited
c) collected
d) processed

6 *before long*
a) shortly
b) rapidly
c) immediately
d) eventually

Unit 11

How lions live

Multiple choice

A passage will either be read to you twice by your teacher or played on a recording. Listen carefully both times and then answer the following questions.
Choose the response which best reflects the meaning of the text.

1 'Membership of a pride is a form of life insurance', because
a) most male lions die a violent death.
b) all members share in the kill.
c) the life of a male is insecure.
d) very few males reach old age.

2 Which of the following is *not* true?
A pride of lions
a) will never go outside its own territory.
b) will kill all animals that enter its territory.
c) will usually live within fixed limits.
d) will often fight for new territory.

3 The author expected the lioness
a) would not come back to her cub.
b) would eat her cub.
c) would show more feeling.
d) would return to feed her cub.

Listening comprehension: Unit 11

4 When a kill is made
a) the adult lions share their portion with the cubs.
b) the cubs have to wait in the bush for their mother to bring them food.
c) there is never any food left for the cubs.
d) the male lions sometimes let the cubs eat with them.

True or false?

Listen to the passage again, then decide whether the following statements are true or false.

1 Female lions are more closely attached to the pride than males.
2 Most male lions die violently.
3 Old males are looked after by the rest of the pride.
4 The pride guards its territory fiercely.
5 The male lion the author found had been fighting over a kill.
6 The author was not surprised at what happened after the lion's death.
7 The dead lion's companion tried to protect her cubs from the attackers.
8 The author had expected the lioness to show some feeling towards her cub.
9 Lionesses make sure that their cubs are well fed.
10 Male lions never let the cubs share in the kill.

Vocabulary in context

How well did you understand the following words or phrases when you heard them? Choose the most accurate definition.

1 *for life*
a) in order to live
b) throughout their lives
c) because they enjoy it
d) to look after the cubs

2 *insecure*
a) dangerous
b) unpleasant
c) short
d) uncertain

3 *intruders*
a) trespassers
b) prey
c) females
d) old lions

4 *take care not to run fast enough*
a) make sure they do not run too fast
b) are unable to run fast enough
c) cannot be bothered to run fast enough
d) have difficulty in running fast enough

Listening comprehension: Unit 11

5 *this is not always the case*
a) lions do not always chase away intruders
b) the intruders are not always allowed to escape
c) lions do not always roar at intruders
d) intruders are not always unwelcome

6 *insight into*
a) dislike of
b) understanding of
c) fear of
d) love of

7 *grief*
a) anger
b) pain
c) sorrow
d) disgust

8 *self-indulgent*
a) greedy
b) self-satisfied
c) proud
d) self-assured

9 *carcass*
a) body
b) intestines
c) limbs
d) flesh

10 *by the time she has done so*
a) by the time the lioness has finished eating
b) by the time the lioness has reached her cubs
c) by the time the lioness has brought her cubs to the kill
d) by the time the lioness has finished cleaning herself

Summary

Consider the reading and listening comprehension texts together. What facts have you learnt about the life of lions? Make use, if you like, of the following sentence-openings:
- Male lions spend less . .
- The hunting is usually done by . . .
- Without the protection of the males, the cubs . . .
- Dusk is the lion's favourite . . .
- Lions have little difficulty . . .
- When hunting . . .
- A male lion is unlikely to reach old age because . . .
- Belonging to the pride is important because ..
- If one lion intrudes upon another's territory . . .
- Lions show little mercy towards . . .
- When an animal is killed . . .
- At feeding time the males sometimes have to . . .

Unit 12

Telepathy

Multiple choice

A passage will either be read to you twice by your teacher or played on a recording.
Listen carefully both times and then answer the following questions.
Choose the response which best reflects the meaning of the text.

1 While the young girl was walking along the lane
a) she suddenly fainted.
b) she thought she saw her mother lying dead on the floor.
c) she had a vision of a white handkerchief.
d) she remembered the day when her mother had died of a heart attack.

2 When the doctor and the girl reached the house
a) the mother was already dead.
b) the mother was recovering from a heart attack.
c) the mother was pretending to have a heart attack.
d) the mother was still suffering from a heart attack.

3 The fact that the child went straight to the doctor proves that
a) the whole story was an invention.
b) she could not have added the details later.
c) she believed in the truth of her vision.
d) her memory could not be trusted.

4 A physician in the *New York Times* Magazine suggested that the child's mother
a) had been pretending to have a heart attack on this occasion.
b) suffered regularly from serious heart attacks.
c) suffered from imaginary heart attacks.
d) suffered from imaginary attacks of hysteria.

5 The speaker does not agree with the physician's suggestion because
a) he thinks the doctor ought to have mentioned that the woman had frequent heart attacks.
b) if the woman did have frequent heart attacks the doctor would have mentioned it.
c) the girl later in life spoke of the vision as a mere exercise of the imagination.
d) the girl was not able to understand her experience.

True or false?

Listen to the passage again, then decide whether the following statements
are true or false.

   1 When she had the vision, the girl was in the centre of town.
   2 When the vision came she lost conciousness.
   3 She thought her mother was dead.

Listening comprehension: Unit 12

4 After the vision she went straight to the doctor.
5 The girl was used to having visions like this.
6 Her mother was pretending to have a heart attack.
7 It is unlikely that the girl invented the story.
8 The girl lied about the handkerchief.
9 The physician who wrote about this case in the *New York Times* Magazine considered the girl's vision to be remarkable.
10 The doctor had mentioned that the woman was subject to frequent heart attacks.
11 Later in life the girl frequently spoke about this incident.

Vocabulary in context

How well did you understand the following words or phrases when you heard them? Choose the most accurate definition.

1 *telepathy*
a) heart disease
b) transference of thought
c) prediction of the future
d) imagination

2 *apparently*
a) seemingly
b) obviously
c) probably
d) certainly

3 *upset*
a) impressed
b) distressed
c) excited
d) puzzled

4 *verified*
a) accepted
b) stated
c) proved
d) believed

5 *discredit*
a) explain
b) support
c) throw fresh light upon
d) bring into question

6 *likely*
a) attractive
b) probable
c) suitable
d) provable

Listening comprehension: Unit 13

7 *subject to*
a) scared of
b) examined because of
c) suffering from
d) resistant to

Unit 13

Atomic cars

Multiple choice

A passage will either be read to you twice by your teacher or played on a recording. Listen carefully both times and then answer the following questions.
Choose the response which best reflects the meaning of the text.

1 There are a number of problems involved in the production of an atomic car. Which of these is *not* one of them?
a) It would be too heavy to move.
b) It would be too expensive to produce.
c) It would be too dangerous to use.
d) It would be too costly to run.

2 The ideal metal for use in atomic cars would be
a) thick, heavy, and cheap.
b) synthetic, strong and thick.
c) thin, light and economical.
d) light, strong and synthetic.

3 The most difficult problem to solve before atomic cars are possible is
a) the cost of production.
b) the prevention of accidents.
c) the invention of new materials.
d) the control of radiation.

4 It will become economically worthwhile to produce an atomic car as soon as
a) all the technical problems have been solved.
b) it becomes too expensive to buy and use petrol.
c) the new type of metal can be produced cheaply enough.
d) the advantages of mass production and savings on fuel are realised.

5 Why would an atomic car need to carry a lot of lead?
a) To prevent the engine from exploding.
b) To stop the car from going too fast.
c) To take the place of the petrol.
d) To protect the people from the rays.

True or false?

Listen to the passage again, then decide whether the following statements are true or false.

Listening comprehension: Unit 13

1 Atomic cars will cost a lot to run.
2 A piece of uranium would last a long time.
3 An atomic engine has already been tried in a car.
4 Radiation is a major problem.
5 It will be necessary to invent a light, impenetrable metal.
6 It will never be possible to produce atomic cars sufficiently cheaply.
7 Accidents between atomic cars would not matter very much.

Vocabulary in context

How well did you understand the following words or phrases when you heard them? Choose the most accurate definition.

1 *outlay*
a) exploitation
b) exemption
c) exaggeration
d) expenditure

2 *harness*
a) utilise
b) unite
c) undertake
d) uncover

3 *conquered*
a) undertaken
b) overlooked
c) overcome
d) undergone

4 *summed up*
a) resumed
b) added together
c) illustrated
d) described

5 *fatal results*
a) resulting in serious damage
b) resulting in death
c) resulting in bad health
d) resulting in injury

6 *impracticable*
a) not feasible
b) not usual
c) not economical
d) not sensible

7 Write down all the facts you can learn from the text about 'lead', 'uranium' and 'synthetic'.

8 The word 'power' is used several times in the extract. Listen carefully for another word which also occurs and means more or less the same.

Listening comprehension: Unit 14

Unit 14

What happens inside a pyramid

Multiple choice

A passage will either be read to you twice by your teacher or played on a recording. Listen carefully both times and then answer the following questions.
Choose the response which best reflects the meaning of the text.

1 The pyramids were built
a) for royal celebrations.
b) as houses for the pharaohs.
c) as shelters from the sun.
d) as tombs for the pharaohs.

2 How did the dead cat and other animals get into the pyramid?
a) Tourists had brought them in.
b) They had come in by chance.
c) They had come in to shelter from the sun.
d) They had belonged to the pharaoh.

3 What surprised Bovis most about the inside of the pyramid?
a) That it was full of rubbish and dead animals.
b) That it was extremely humid.
c) That the animals had not decayed.
d) That the mummies had been so carefully embalmed.

4 Bovis began to wonder whether
a) it was the humidity which helped preserve dead bodies.
b) the pyramid shape had something to do with mummification.
c) it was their subjects who had embalmed the pharaohs.
d) the pharaohs had been carelessly embalmed.

5 What did Bovis do to test his idea?
a) He put a dead cat in the Cheops pyramid.
b) He tried putting a razor under his model pyramid.
c) He put a dead cat in a replica of the Cheops pyramid.
d) He got in touch with a radio engineer in Prague.

6 When Drbal put his used razor in the model pyramid
a) it became blunt.
b) nothing happened.
c) it became sharp.
d) it became rusty.

7 The speaker thinks that the cardboard model of a pyramid
a) is not much good for preserving food.
b) is just a random arrangement of pieces of cardboard.
c) has some mysterious special properties.
d) preserves food better than a shoe-box.

Listening comprehension: Unit 14

True or false?

Listen to the passage again, then decide whether the following statements are true or false.

1 The pyramids were royal palaces.
2 The smallest pyramid is called Cheops.
3 It was rather humid inside the pyramid.
4 Bovis met a group of tourists in the pyramid.
5 The dead cat and the other animals became mummified because of the humidity.
6 Bovis suspected that it was the pyramids which dehydrated and preserved dead bodies.
7 Bovis put a dead cat inside the Cheops pyramid.
8 Karel Drbal did the same experiment as Bovis.
9 Drbal concluded that a shape does not influence the processes going on inside it.
10 The superstition said that the moon sharpened razor-blades.
11 The objects inside the model pyramid soon began to smell.
12 The author thinks there is something special about the properties of a pyramid.

Vocabulary in context

How well did you understand the following words or phrases when you heard them? Choose the most accurate definition.

1 *humid*
a) rather hot
b) rather wet
c) rather cool
d) rather dry

2 *garbage*
a) dead animals
b) rubbish
c) humidity
d) tourists

3 The word 'embalmed' occurs in the passage. So does *one* of the following words which means roughly the same.
a) humified
b) horrified
c) mollified
d) mummified

4 The word 'litter' occurs in the passage. One of the following words also occurs and means roughly the same.
a) cabbage
b) baggage
c) garbage
d) luggage

Listening comprehension: Unit 14

5 'Dehydration' occurs, and so does *one* of these phrases, which means the same.
a) dried out
b) tied up
c) lined up
d) tried out

6 'Sharp' occurs, and so does *one* of these words, which means the *opposite*.
a) bright
b) blunt
c) soft
d) damp

7 Which of the following is an example of a 'superstition'?
a) Breaking a mirror is unlucky.
b) Eating garlic makes your breath smell.
c) Getting up early is good for you.
d) Being kind to people is worthwhile.

8 If you saw someone coughing and sneezing, what would you 'conclude'?

9 The phrase 'an accurate scale model' occurs, and so does *one* of these words, which means the same.
a) imitation
b) copy
c) representation
d) replica

10 Which of these two arrangements of dots is a 'random arrangement'?

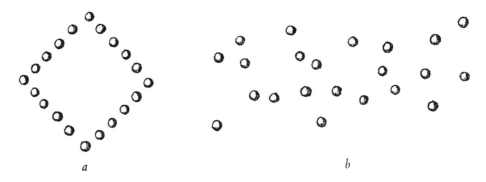

a   b

11 The word 'decayed' occurs in the passage. So does *one* of the following words, which means the *opposite*.

a) reserved
b) preserved
c) deterred
d) conferred

Unit 15

Up the creek

Multiple choice

A passage will either be read to you twice by your teacher or played on a recording. Listen carefully both times and then answer the following questions. Choose the response which best reflects the meaning of the text.

1 There are some features of Western culture which are present in West Africa.
a) This fact makes it easier to accept the unfamiliarity of West Africa.
b) This fact makes West Africa seem even stranger.
c) This fact makes no difference to our reaction to West Africa.
d) This fact has been greatly overemphasised.

2 The most frightening landscapes in the world are
a) in Norway.
b) in Upper Provence.
c) in West Africa.
d) in the Alps.

3 A lot of the old African religion has to do with
a) kidnapping people.
b) keeping the spirits awake.
c) human sacrifice.
d) keeping the spirits happy.

4 The author was kept awake by
a) a ghost.
b) his friend.
c) the witches.
d) eerie feelings.

5 'Mangrove' means
a) a sort of bird.
b) a sort of man.
c) a sort of tree.
d) a sort of animal.

True or false?

Listen to the passage again, then decide whether the following statements are true or false.

1 African life has lost its unfamiliarity.
2 Most countries do not have frightening landscapes.
3 West Africa has more weird regions than anywhere else.
4 These landscapes frighten foreigners only.
5 African religions believe in ghosts.
6 The author thought he would be eaten by witches.

Listening comprehension: Unit 16

7 It was very quiet in the creeks of the Niger delta.
8 He was on a visit to Lagos.
9 The port was very modern.
10 It was easy to get off the canoe.

Vocabulary in context

1 Which of these words from the passage mean more or less the same as 'weird'?
a) wild
b) unknown
c) strange
d) lonely

2 Which of these phrases from the passage mean more or less the same as 'eerie regions'?
a) vistas secret, interminable and somehow meaningless
b) landscapes that arouse unease
c) evil spirits which live in a particular tree or a particular rock
d) an area of black mud and tumbled blocks of stone

3 *placating* means
a) finding out about
b) keeping happy
c) looking after
d) keeping awake

4 *derelict* means
a) old-fashioned
b) enormous
c) slippery
d) disused

Summary

Now you will hear the tape again. This time make careful notes, then write a summary of the text from your notes.

Unit 16

The year 2000

Multiple choice

A passage will either be read to you twice by your teacher or played on a recording. Listen carefully both times and then answer the following questions.
Choose the response which best reflects the meaning of the text.

1 By the year 2000 the world economy will have grown by
a) five times.
b) 500 per cent.
c) an unknown amount
d) 50 per cent.

Listening comprehension: Unit 17

2 World petrol reserves will be used up by 1985 if
a) Western European consumption continues to expand.
b) South-East Asia does not limit its consumption.
c) underdeveloped countries start to use petrol at the same rate as Westen Europe.
d) world population continues to expand.

3 The speaker thinks that we should
a) do nothing.
b) act now.
c) wait ten years.
d) wait twenty years.

4 If we act immediately, the world's population
a) could stabilise in thirty-five years' time.
b) would not stop growing.
c) would stop growing in about fifty years' time.
d) could stabilise in about seventy-five years' time.

5 If we do nothing
a) it will cost us a lot of money.
b) it will be the most natural solution.
c) the death-rate will rise dramatically.
d) the practical problems will become clear.

True or false?

Listen to the passage again, then decide whether the following statements are true or false.

1 There will certainly not be enough raw materials for the world economy in the year 2000.
2 World petrol supplies will be exhausted by 1985.
3 We need to use natural resources carefully and divide them up equally.
4 Expansion of population will be greatest in the Southern Hemisphere.
5 If nothing is done, the population will expand enormously.
6 If we act in 1975, population growth could be brought under control within seventy-five years.
7 The longer we wait to act, the better it will be.
8 The solution to the problem should be left to nature.

Unit 17

Learning to speak

Multiple choice

A passage will either be read to you twice by your teacher or played on a recording. Listen carefully both times and then answer the following questions. Choose the response which best reflects the meaning of the text.

Listening comprehension: Unit 17

1 Children who start speaking late
a) may have problems with their hearing.
b) probably do not hear enough language spoken around them.
c) usually pay close attention to what they hear.
d) often take a long time in learning to listen properly.

2 A baby's first noises are
a) a reflection of his moods and feelings.
b) an early form of language.
c) a sign that he means to tell you something.
d) an imitation of the speech of adults.

3 The problem of deciding at what point a baby's imitations can be considered as speech
a) is important because words have different meanings for different people.
b) is not especially important because the changeover takes place gradually.
c) is one that can never be properly understood because the meaning of words changes with age.
d) is one that should be completely ignored because children's use of words is often meaningless.

4 The speaker implies that
a) parents can never hope to teach their children new sounds.
b) children no longer imitate people after they begin to speak.
c) children who are good at imitating learn new sounds more quickly.
d) even after they have learnt to speak children still enjoy imitating.

True or false?

Listen to the passage again, then decide whether the following statements are true or false.

1 The speaker cannot explain how a child manages to learn to speak so quickly.
2 Before they begin to speak most children do about the same amount of listening.
3 Children dislike obeying instructions.
4 Children can ask questions by making noises.
5 Children first imitate adults, then themselves.
6 Words do not have fixed meanings.
7 Children's first words are usually meaningless because they can apply to many different things.

Vocabulary in context

How well did you understand the following words or phrases when you heard them? Choose the most accurate definition.

1 *vary*
a) worry
b) differ
c) develop
d) change

Listening comprehension: Unit 18

2 *sort themselves out*
a) become evident
b) are learnt
c) are discovered
d) take the place of others

3 *it is agreed*
a) it has been proved
b) it is generally accepted
c) it is obvious
d) it is most likely

4 *cash in on*
a) ignore
b) exploit
c) discourage
d) praise

Unit 18

Tiny killers on the march

Multiple choice

A passage will either be read to you twice by your teacher or played on a recording. Listen carefully both times and then answer the following questions. Choose the response which best reflects the meaning of the text.

1 Soldier ants are
a) extremely aggressive.
b) fierce only when attacked.
c) too slow to be really dangerous.
d) vicious, but easily frightened.

2 The author's main purpose was to
a) photograph the Queen ant.
b) discover why soldier ants attack people who collapse near their nests.
c) study the habits of soldier ants.
d) kill the soldier ants.

3 'The soldier ants formed the flanks' means
a) the soldier ants waited while the worker ants passed.
b) the soldier ants came behind the worker ants.
c) the soldier ants were on either side of the worker ants.
d) the soldier ants formed a separate column.

4 When the Queen ant appeared, the author
a) tried to photograph her, but without success.
b) immediately dropped his camera.

Listening comprehension: Unit 18

c) managed to take a few pictures.
d) was unable to take pictures because of the soldier ants.

True or false?

Listen to the passage again, then decide whether the following statements are true or false.

1 The author was told of a rat which had been eaten to death by soldier ants.
2 Soldier ants will eat human beings.
3 Soldier ants build their nests in rivers.
4 It is easy to tell where soldier ants have built their nests.
5 After the males have fertilised the Queen's eggs they are killed by her.
6 The Queen never travels by day.
7 The author had been observing the same ants' nest for more than two weeks.
8 When soldier ants travel they move in a column ten feet wide.
9 The ants do not bring out the larvae until they feel safe.
10 The author did not have time to photograph the Queen.
11 A man can be driven mad by the bite of a soldier ant.

Vocabulary in context

How well did you understand the following words or phrases when you heard them? Choose the most accurate definition.

1 *blunder into*
a) run into accidentally
b) run into aggressively
c) run into carefully
d) run into frequently

2 *indentations*
a) small cracks
b) small bumps
c) small heaps
d) small depressions

3 *keeps court*
a) is imprisoned
b) rules
c) keeps out of the way
d) hides

4 *escorted*
a) accompanied
b) pursued
c) attacked
d) prevented

Listening comprehension: Unit 19

5 *about to move*
a) preparing to leave
b) prevented from going
c) moving about
d) on their way

6 *surge*
a) noise
b) wave
c) sense
d) change

7 *exposures*
a) slaps
b) steps
c) pictures
d) bites

8 *leap*
a) jump
b) crawl
c) fall
d) slip

Unit 19

Sensory deprivation in space

Multiple choice

A passage will either be read to you twice by your teacher or played on a recording. Listen carefully both times and then answer the following questions.
Choose the response which best reflects the meaning of the text.

1 The experiment described was intended to find out what happens when people
a) sleep for too long.
b) are put in a novel situation.
c) are cut off from all sensations.
d) want to become astronauts.

2 The experimenters knew how long subjects slept because
a) they could watch them.
b) the subjects told them.
c) they had long experience.
d) they could hear them.

3 The experimenters were surprised by the long period of sleep because the subjects
a) should have been interested in their new experience.
b) had all been asleep already.

Listening comprehension: Unit 19

c) should have experienced hallucinations.
d) had no real sensations to work on.

4 Many subjects saw things which were not there because
a) their brains invented sensations to fill the gap left by SD.
b) they were ready to believe anything.
c) the experimenters influenced them with changing lights and sounds.
d) they were highly impressionable people.

5 The experimenters started to put their subjects in SD in the early morning because
a) they were surprised by their earlier reactions.
b) they wanted them to dissipate the effects of SD.
c) they wanted them to get the maximum effect from SD.
d) it made no difference when the experiment was started.

True or false?

Listen to the passage again, then decide whether the following statements are true or false.

1 The experiments described were to find out how long people sleep.
2 Subjects knew for certain how long they had slept.
3 Most of the people undergoing the experiment slept for most of the first day.
4 When people were put in SD in the morning, they did not sleep so long.
5 The experimenters were not surprised by their results.
6 SD should not have put the subjects to sleep.
7 Yuri Gagarin did not sleep during his space flight.
8 Sleeping was the only effect of SD.
9 When the brain has no real sensations to occupy it, it invents imaginary ones.
10 It is easy to influence people who have just experienced SD.

Vocabulary in context

How well did you understand the following words or phrases when you heard them? Choose the most accurate definition.

1 *gross*
a) rude
b) rough
c) accurate
d) big

2 *elapse*
a) pass
b) stop
c) change
d) disappear

3 *a nap*
a) a deep sleep
b) a short sleep

Listening comprehension: Unit 20

c) a bad sleep
d) a bad dream

4 *dissipate*
a) prevent
b) strengthen
c) lessen
d) avoid

5 *hallucinations* refer to
a) having daydreams
b) seeing things very clearly
c) having no real sensations
d) seeing things which are not there

Unit 20

A near-disaster in space

Multiple choice

A passage will either be read to you twice by your teacher or played on a recording. Listen carefully both times and then answer the following questions.
Choose the response which best reflects the meaning of the text.

1 1967 was
a) a good year for the Russians and the Americans.
b) a good year for the Americans but not for the Russians.
c) a bad year for the Americans and the Russians.
d) a bad year for the Americans but not for the Russians.

2 A number of accidents happened in 1967. Choose the one which did *not* happen. The astronauts were
a) burnt to death.
b) left lost in space.
c) killed when the parachute did not open.

3 Why was the breakdown of the oxygen supply so important?
a) Because it could cause an explosion.
b) Because they could not fire their rocket without it.
c) Because they never found out the reason for it.
d) Because it affected all the systems in the module.

4 The astronauts survived because
a) the command module was not very badly damaged.
b) the lunar module was intended as a lifeboat.
c) they managed to improvise.
d) they had read a lot of adventure stories.

Listening comprehension: Unit 20

5 How did the astronauts get back into the atmosphere from space?
a) By using a parachute.
b) By going back into the command module.
c) By staying in the service module.
d) By burning the lunar module.

True or false?

Listen to the passage again, then decide whether the following statements are true or false.

1 No one is surprised that few space accidents have taken place.
2 The Americans lost an astronaut when his parachute did not open.
3 People expected that some day astronauts would be left in space.
4 Some astronauts were stranded in space in 1970.
5 The cause of the accident was engine failure.
6 The oxygen was used for many different purposes.
7 The astronauts were ingenious.
8 Makeshift repairs are impossible in space.
9 The spacecraft was on a trajectory which would have brought it back to earth.
10 Life for the astronauts in Apollo 13 was unbearable.
11 The heat-shield of the command module had been damaged by the explosion.

Vocabulary in context

How well did you understand the following words or phrases when you heard them? Choose the most accurate definition.

1 *fatal*
a) causing injury
b) causing death
c) causing illness
d) causing failure

2 *stranded*
a) delayed
b) isolated
c) injured
d) killed

3 *jettison*
a) get off
b) turn over
c) throw away
d) break open

4 *makeshift*
a) expensive
b) elaborate
c) technical
d) improvised

Listening comprehension: Unit 20

5 *wits*
a) endurance
b) experience
c) intelligence
d) connections

6 *ruled out*
a) ruined
b) excluded
c) improved
d) justified

7 Which of these pictures shows a *parachute*?

a   b   c

8 Which of these keys is the *duplicate* of the one on the left?

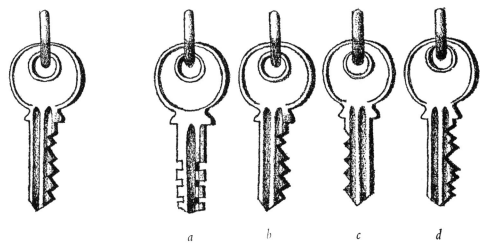

a   b   c   d

9 Which of the following words used in the passage have a similar meaning?
a) adapt
b) repair
c) convert
d) avoid

10 Which line shows an *orbit*?

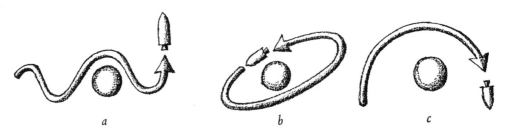

a   b   c

11 Which of these lines shows a *trajectory*?

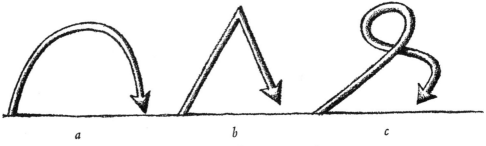

a   b   c

12 'Intelligence and the ability to use limited resources . . .'
This phrase is summed up by *one* of the following words in the passage:
a) ingenuousness
b) ingenuity
c) induction
d) engineering

13 People who 'convert bits of wreckage into a raft . . . and make a bow and arrow from branches and bootlaces . . .' are showing evidence of:
a) inability
b) improvement
c) improvidence
d) improvisation